HUNTERS OF THE NORTHERN FOREST

TIME®
LIFE
BOOKS

Other Publications:
THE TIME-LIFE COMPLETE GARDENER
THE NEW HOME REPAIR AND IMPROVEMENT
JOURNEY THROUGH THE MIND AND BODY
WEIGHT WATCHERS ®SMART CHOICE RECIPE COLLECTION
TRUE CRIME
THE ART OF WOODWORKING
LOST CIVILIZATIONS
ECHOES OF GLORY
THE NEW FACE OF WAR
HOW THINGS WORK
WINGS OF WAR
CREATIVE EVERYDAY COOKING
COLLECTOR'S LIBRARY OF THE UNKNOWN
CLASSICS OF WORLD WAR II
TIME-LIFE LIBRARY OF CURIOUS AND UNUSUAL FACTS
AMERICAN COUNTRY
VOYAGE THROUGH THE UNIVERSE
THE THIRD REICH
MYSTERIES OF THE UNKNOWN
TIME FRAME
FIX IT YOURSELF
FITNESS, HEALTH & NUTRITION
SUCCESSFUL PARENTING
HEALTHY HOME COOKING
UNDERSTANDING COMPUTERS
LIBRARY OF NATIONS
THE ENCHANTED WORLD
THE KODAK LIBRARY OF CREATIVE PHOTOGRAPHY
GREAT MEALS IN MINUTES
THE CIVIL WAR
PLANET EARTH
COLLECTOR'S LIBRARY OF THE CIVIL WAR
THE EPIC OF FLIGHT
THE GOOD COOK
WORLD WAR II
THE OLD WEST

For information on and a full description of any of the Time-Life Books series listed above, please call 1-800-621-7026 or write:
Reader Information
Time-Life Customer Service
P.O. Box C-32068
Richmond, Virginia 23261-2068

This volume is one of a series that chronicles the history and culture of the Native Americans. Other books in the series include:

THE FIRST AMERICANS
THE SPIRIT WORLD
THE EUROPEAN CHALLENGE
PEOPLE OF THE DESERT
THE WAY OF THE WARRIOR
THE BUFFALO HUNTERS
REALM OF THE IROQUOIS
THE MIGHTY CHIEFTAINS
KEEPERS OF THE TOTEM

CYCLES OF LIFE
WAR FOR THE PLAINS
TRIBES OF THE SOUTHERN WOODLANDS
THE INDIANS OF CALIFORNIA
PEOPLE OF THE ICE AND SNOW
PEOPLE OF THE LAKES
THE WOMAN'S WAY
PEOPLE OF THE WESTERN RANGE

The Cover: A Slavey man on snowshoes selects a sapling to use with a trap to catch marten near Trout Lake in the boreal forest of northwestern Canada. Although the Slavey began supplying pelts for the fur trade in the 18th century, they remained largely free from European influence until the early 1900s when a rapid rise in fur prices drove many bands to give up their nomadic hunting, fishing, and gathering ways in favor of trapping furbearing animals in order to earn income to buy trade goods.

HUNTERS OF THE NORTHERN FOREST

✤

by
THE EDITORS
of
TIME-LIFE BOOKS

ALEXANDRIA, VIRGINIA

Time-Life Books is a division of Time Life Inc.

PRESIDENT and CEO: John M. Fahey Jr.
EDITOR-IN-CHIEF: John L. Papanek

TIME-LIFE BOOKS

MANAGING EDITOR: Roberta Conlan

Director of Design: Michael Hentges
Director of Editorial Operations: Ellen Robling
Director of Photography and Research: John Conrad Weiser
Senior Editors: Russell B. Adams Jr., Dale M. Brown, Janet Cave, Lee Hassig, Robert Somerville, Henry Woodhead
Special Projects Editor: Rita Thievon Mullin
Director of Technology: Eileen Bradley
Library: Louise D. Forstall

PRESIDENT: John D. Hall

Vice President, Director of Marketing: Nancy K. Jones
Vice President, Director of New Product Development: Neil Kagan
Vice President, Book Production: Marjann Caldwell
Production Manager: Marlene Zack
Quality Assurance Manager: Miriam P. Newton

THE AMERICAN INDIANS

SERIES EDITOR: Henry Woodhead
Administrative Editor: Loretta Y. Britten

Editorial Staff for *Hunters of the Northern Forest*
Senior Art Director: Ray Ripper
Picture Editor: Susie Kelly
Text Editors: John Newton (principal), Stephen G. Hyslop
Associate Editors/Research-Writing: Mary Helena McCarthy (principal), Trudy W. Pearson, Jennifer Veech
Senior Copyeditor: Ann Lee Bruen
Picture Coordinator: Daryl Beard
Editorial Assistant: Christine Higgins

Special Contributors: Maggie Debelius, Tom Lewis, Michelle Murphy, Carl Posey (text); Marilyn Murphy Terrell (research-writing); Martha Lee Beckington, Christian Kinney, Dean Nadalin (research); Barbara L. Klein (index).

Correspondents: Christine Hinze (London), Christina Lieberman (New York), Maria Vincenza Aloisi (Paris), Ann Natanson (Rome). Valuable assistance was also provided by: Barbara Gevene Hertz (Copenhagen), Elizabeth Brown (New York), Carolyn Sackett (Seattle).

General Consultants
Robert Brightman is associate professor of anthropology and linguistics at Reed College in Portland, Oregon. He has done extensive research on subarctic Algonquian cultures and has written several books, including *Grateful Prey: Rock Cree Human-Animal Relationships.* Dr. Brightman also coauthored *"The Orders of the Dreamed,"* a collection of letters and journals of an early-19th-century anglo-Canadian fur trapper who observed Cree and Northern Ojibwa religion and myth.

Frederick E. Hoxie is academic vice president for the Newberry Library in Chicago and former director of its D'Arcy McNickle Center for the History of the American Indian. Dr. Hoxie is the author of *A Final Promise: The Campaign to Assimilate the Indians 1880-1920* and other works. He has served as a history consultant to the Cheyenne River and Standing Rock Sioux tribes, Little Big Horn College archives, and the Senate Select Committee on Indian Affairs. He is a trustee of the National Museum of the American Indian in Washington, D.C.

Adrian Tanner is professor of anthropology at Memorial University, St John's, Newfoundland, where he has taught since 1972. He had his first experience with northern aboriginal peoples in 1957 and has lived among Indians in the Yukon, northern Ontario, northern Quebec, and Labrador. He is the author of the book *Bringing Home Animals* about Cree hunting rituals, and he edited *The Politics of Indianness.* He has written numerous articles and reports on aboriginal land claims, ethnic politics among northern Indians, and social impact assessment and has also given expert testimony in several court cases. Most recently he coauthored a study for the Canadian Royal Commission on Aboriginal Peoples.

First printing. Printed in U.S.A.
Published simultaneously in Canada.
School and library distribution by Time-Life Education, P.O. Box 85026, Richmond, Virginia 23285-5026.
Time-Life is a trademark of Time Warner Inc. U.S.A.

Library of Congress Cataloging in Publication Data
Hunters of the northern forest/by the editors of Time-Life Books.
    p.   cm.—(The American Indians)
Includes bibliographical references and index.
ISBN 0-8094-9570-8
    1. North America—Canada—History. 2. Indians of North America—Canada—Social life and customs. 3. Indians of North America—Alaska—History. 4. Indians of North America—Alaska—Social life and customs. I. Time-Life Books. II. Series.
E78.C2H85 1995   95-5374
971'.00497—dc20   CIP

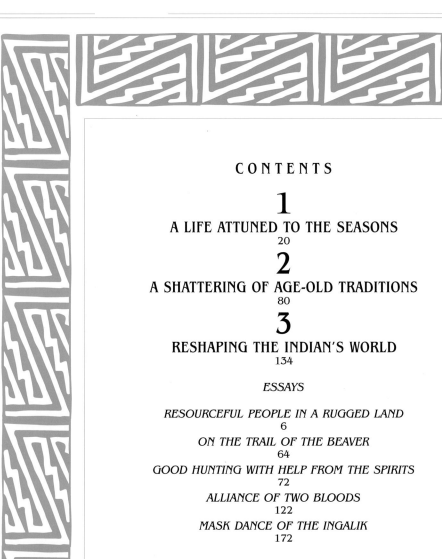

CONTENTS

1
A LIFE ATTUNED TO THE SEASONS

2
A SHATTERING OF AGE-OLD TRADITIONS

3
RESHAPING THE INDIAN'S WORLD

ESSAYS

RESOURCEFUL PEOPLE IN A RUGGED LAND

In 1534, when the French explorer Jacques Cartier first sailed along the mountainous coast of present-day Labrador, he marveled that human beings could survive in such an inhospitable wilderness. "It is not to be called the New Land," he observed, "but rather stones and wild crags, and a place fit for wild beasts, for in all the North Island I did not see a cart load of good earth. There is nothing else but moss and small thorns scattered here and there, withered and dry. To be short, I believe that this was the land that God allotted to Cain."

But survive they did. Thousands of years before the arrival of the Europeans, bands of nomadic hunters developed an intimate knowledge of animals and ingenious technologies, such as the snowshoe, the toboggan, and the bark canoe, that allowed them to live not only in Labrador but all across the geographical and cultural area known today as the North American subarctic.

It is a region of immensity, lying, as its name implies, directly below the Arctic Circle and encompassing most of northern Canada and central Alaska. Much of the land is carpeted by taiga, or coniferous evergreen forest, that is broken up here and there by a multitude of rivers, lakes, and ponds, as well as open swampland and tundra. In the far west, the Canadian Rockies, the Yukon Plateau, the British Columbia Plateau, and other highlands dominate the terrain. The summers are short and bug-filled; the winters are long and fierce, with bone-chilling temperatures and heavy snows that blanket much of the region for more than 200 days of the year.

Although the eastern bands spoke dialects of Algonquian and the western bands Athapaskan tongues, all subarctic Indians enjoyed close ties with the land and its animals, principally the caribou and the moose, which provided most of their food and clothing. After the arrival of the Europeans, many bands traded the pelts of beaver and other furred animals for guns, metal goods, cloth, and various manufactured products. The cold climate and lack of arable soil saved the Indians from displacement by white farmers. Today, many subarctic people remain on their ancestral lands, hunting, fishing, and trapping as they have always done for at least part of every year. A modern Hare Indian from Fort Good Hope in northwest Canada explains: "This land is just like our blood because we live off the animals that feed off the land."

Tanana mailmen and their dog teams prepare to make their rounds in central Alaska in the early 1900s. The tallest peak in North America, 20,270-foot Mount McKinley (right), towers over the area south of the traditional Tanana hunting grounds.

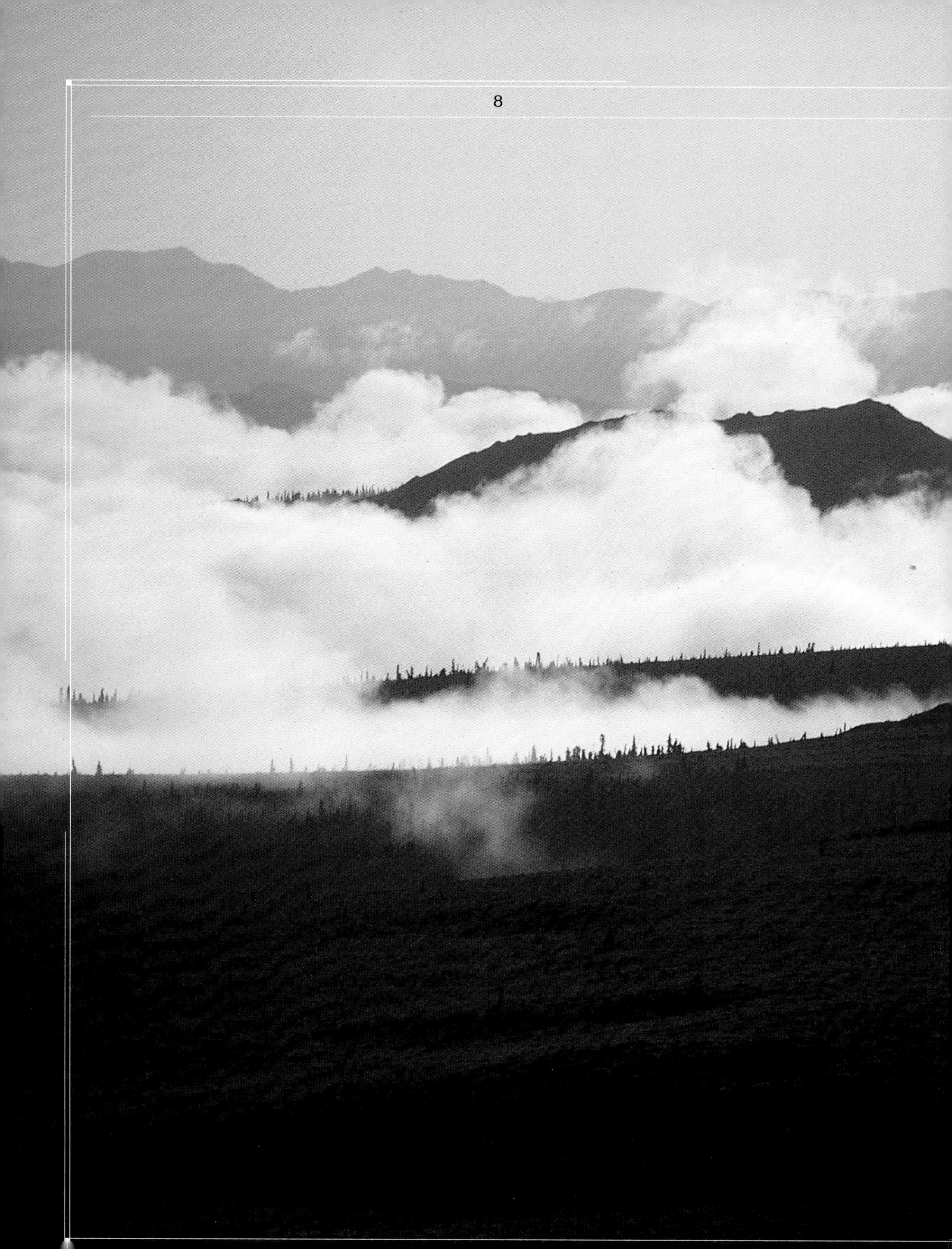

The leader of the Klondike band of Han Indians stands in front of his tent holding a bow and wearing a decorated quiver in this picture taken in 1898. The Han inhabited the Yukon River valley, shown in the large photograph shrouded in billowy clouds.

A Slavey man poses with his pack dogs in western Canada's Hay River country in 1921. The Hay flows into Great Slave Lake, where the Slavey bands gathered in summer. Major game for the Slavey was woodland caribou, a herd of which is shown dashing across a frozen lake.

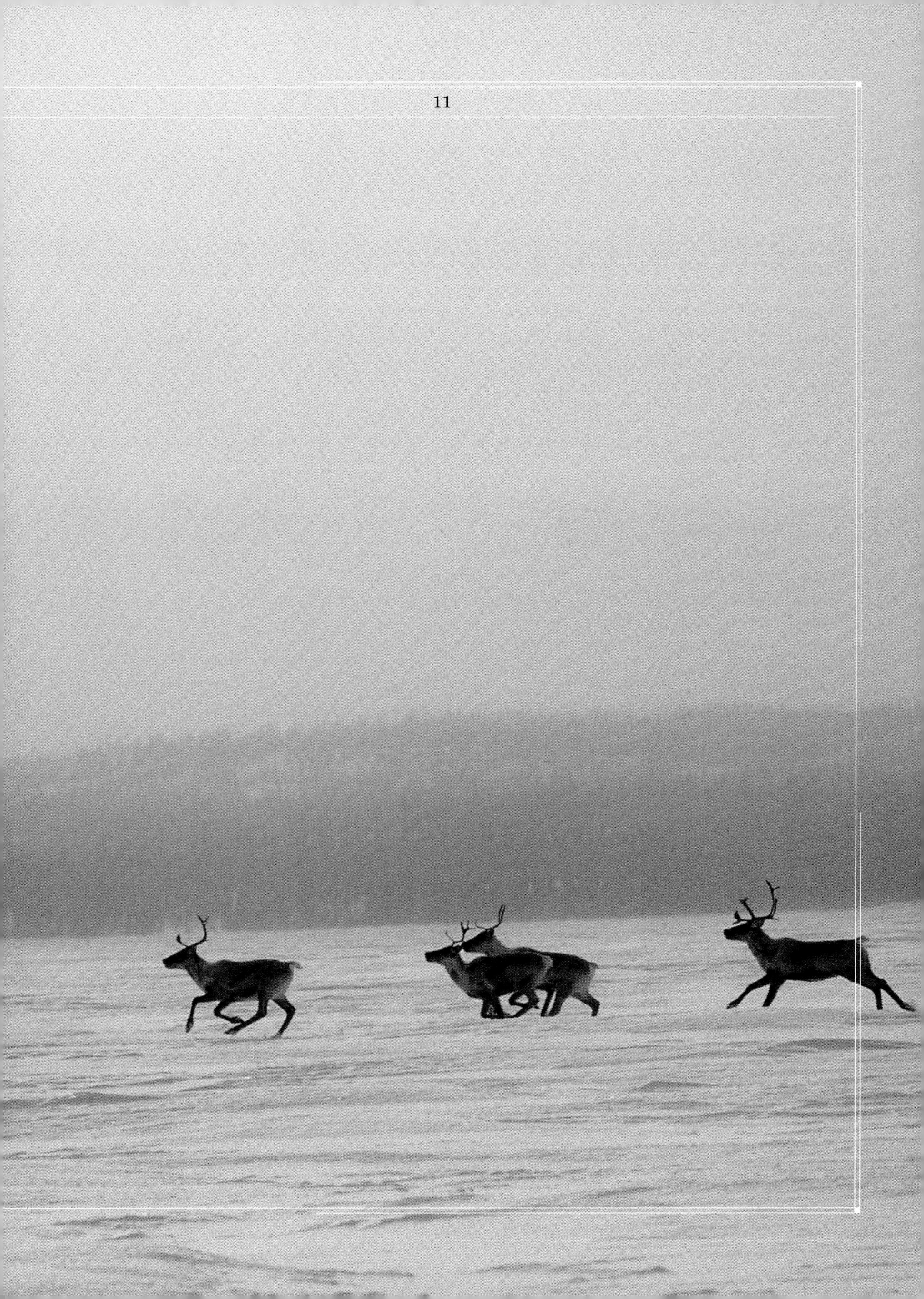

A Carrier man from the Ulkatcho band cleans a moose hide with an ancient tool—a stone scraper tied inside the end of a split stick. The Carrier Indians are native to British Columbia's mountainous interior, typified by the river valley shown here.

Northern Ojibwas from the Island Lake band gather at a hunting camp circa 1925. The seated women and children are wearing woven rabbit-skin jackets. The landscape shows a grove of wind-swept trees in Manitoba—part of the Northern Ojibwa hunting range.

In an 1888 photograph, a Cree family camped along the La Grande River stands beside its hide-covered conical wigwam and birch-bark canoe near Fort George, Quebec. In the landscape, a spectacular sunset reflects off James Bay at low tide, in the vicinity of the Cree hunting grounds near the mouth of the La Grande.

Smoking his stone pipe and wearing mittens strung around his neck, a Naskapi man rests from his labors on a crate of goods. In the large photograph, two bull moose cross a river in Labrador, domain of the Naskapi Indians. Moose remain one of their major game animals.

1

A LIFE ATTUNED TO THE SEASONS

Gathered at a hunting camp along the Bell River in Quebec, Waswanipi Cree children proudly display ducks shot by the teenager standing behind them. The Waswanipi believe that the souls of game animals are reborn so that those killed are always replenished.

For hours the Cree hunter had stalked the moose through the shadows dappling the black spruce forest, keeping downwind of the animal's trail, striding on flat, tapered snowshoes. The bent-birch frames laced with strips of caribou hide permitted him to ride the thin crust that firmed the powdery snow—a crust that was too weak to support the heavy moose, as it foraged for scant winter fodder through drifts that occasionally reached as high as its shoulders. Food was sometimes scarce in the boreal forest, or taiga, of northern Canada. The hunter had traveled hungry for two nights, as he would have described it, for in this cold, dark winter land, the Indians reckoned diurnal time in nights, as they reckoned years in winters.

The Cree's hunting band, an assemblage of several families composed of perhaps a score of people, waited anxiously for him to return and relieve their hunger. During the season of intense cold, the energy required to stay alive was so great that, as the Indian expression had it, a man could "starve to death on rabbits." At times the severe winters made hunting so difficult that there was much less to eat than the lean and angular snowshoe hare that the Indians caught in nets and snares. Under normal conditions, the fall hunt provided enough smoke-dried meat for them to live on. In addition, the hunters planned for the season by locating beaver lodges in order to harvest the fat-rich animals in midwinter when their flesh provided the most nutrition. But in some years, such as this one, game shortages caused the band to live under the threat of famine. In the absence of fresh or cached meat, the band survived on pemmican, the dried meat pounded into flakes and mixed with melted fat and sometimes berries that many Native Americans made. When times were especially lean, there might be only a thin broth of boiled animal dung or willow bark, a pinch of lichen, or a length of caribou hide to chew. Hunger was a feature of life in the northland and the search for food the main preoccupation. Perhaps it was because of this that, as the Cree hunter followed the moose, he was himself tracked by the monster generally known as Windigo.

Windigo appears in many different forms, but usually it is depicted as a giant with a heart of ice, bulging eyes, and a lipless mouth gleaming with long, jagged teeth. Moving sometimes as a monstrous entity, sometimes as a whirlwind, this phantom of hunger haunted the northern woods in winter. As the Cree people hunted moose, caribou, beaver, and bear, so did Windigo hunt Cree men, women, and children. Whenever a hunter failed to return to camp or a child disappeared, it was assumed that Windigo had devoured another victim.

But Windigo was much more than a disturbing presence in the Indians' spirit world—it represented terrible hunger and the cruel choices that hunger forced on people who were desperate for survival, the manifestation of something dark and unspeakable in human need. For all of the Indians' sophisticated knowledge of their environment and hunting know-how, there were times in the forest when starvation hovered close at hand and human flesh was looked upon as the alternative to a lingering death. Succumbing to this temptation, however, carried a terrible consequence: The cannibal developed a bloodlust; he or she "turned Windigo," as the Indians said, and had to be driven away from the band or killed.

Snowshoes enable these hunters to pursue buffalo without bogging down in an 1825 painting by explorer Peter Rindisbacher. An observer who spent one winter at a Naskapi camp noted, "An Indian without snowshoes in winter is as helpless as a steamship without its engine."

For this particular Cree hunter, the specter of starvation began to evaporate when he came upon the broken snow marking the passage of a foraging moose. After feeding on willow twigs, the animal had doubled back on its trail and lain down to rest, as it habitually did, with its nose pointed into the wind so it could scent any following predators. The moose would behave exactly as the hunter's guardian spirit had revealed to him many winters ago.

The guardian spirit, himself a moose, had visited the hunter in the form of a human body in a dream when the man was still a boy. It had told him the ways of the large-antlered animals so that he might hunt them when he got older. In addition, a moose had appeared in the hunter's dreams a few nights earlier, a sure signal that the hunt would be successful. Now, following the teachings of his spirit helper, the hunter stalked into the wind until he could scent the moose where it lay ahead of him in the snow. He gripped his birch bow horizontally, his fingers holding a trio of birch arrows fletched with duck feathers; one arrow was notched on the taut bowstring of twisted caribou gut. He saw the great animal then, its antlers splendid, its warm body wreathed in steam. The hunter stole so close that the moose could hear him. The enormous creature lumbered to

An Athapaskan hunter prepares to plunge his knife into a moose in this 19th-century engraving. Because moose are not quick swimmers, swift-paddling hunters were able to overtake the animals and dispatch them with knife or spear.

its feet, stood for a moment in its snow bed; then it turned to face the threat. In that gesture, in that turning toward the fatal arrow, the animal gave itself to the man.

This self-offering by the animal was the dominant spiritual explanation for the hunter's ability to find and kill animals. They were jittery and shy of human company and could conceal themselves against their forest background; they possessed manifest intelligence and, often, greater size and strength. It was inconceivable that the beaver, so adept at building lodges and damming streams, could be tricked by humans. How else could the black bear, so human in form and cunning in behavior, be lured from hibernation? How could it be killed without its cooperation?

Clearly, there was no greater gift than that of the animal to the hunter. For his part, this hunter would skin, gut, and dismember the moose with ceremonial care—to leave its blood on the snow risked bringing a track-obliterating blizzard—and cache it in a spot where even the wolverine could not find it. Initially, he would take only the heart and some other token parts, so that when he returned to camp, his wife would see that he had found large game. Subsequently, the entire camp would move to the kill site, and the hunter would retrieve his cache and honor one of his fellows, perhaps one who had been less fortunate in the hunt, by giving him the meat and organs to distribute among the band as well as to share with any visitors to their camp. The hunter would see to it that the remains were treated with respect. Everyone knew that a hunter who treated his prey as anything less than an honored equal would soon find himself with nothing to hunt. As for the great elongated skull and rack of antlers, the hunter would place them in a tree for his animal friend, where the departed moose might watch the sunrise and reassure other moose that they need not be afraid to yield their bodies to men.

Such reciprocations between man and animal are elements in an age-less tapestry of behavior and belief that links Native Americans across the sub-arctic. Their domain is a two-million-square-mile belt of previously glaciated land extending from Labrador to Alaska, and from the plains of southern Canada to

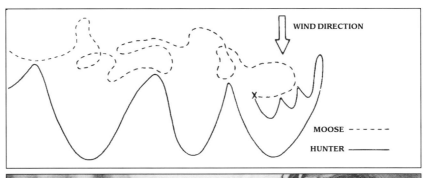

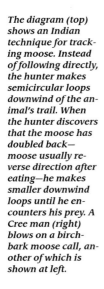

The diagram (top) shows an Indian technique for tracking moose. Instead of following directly, the hunter makes semicircular loops downwind of the animal's trail. When the hunter discovers that the moose has doubled back—moose usually reverse direction after eating—he makes smaller downwind loops until he encounters his prey. A Cree man (right) blows on a birchbark moose call, another of which is shown at left.

the tundra bordering the Arctic. They are the people of the northern forest, hunters of the big game that waxes and wanes with the seasons.

Although they formed many different groups, the subarctic peoples never possessed the political and economic gravitation needed to coalesce into the larger societies of tribes and nations. Their total population has always been limited—one estimate places it at 60,000 at the time of the first substantive European contact during the early 16th century. In an environment too cold for agriculture (the region averages only 40 to 60 frost-free days a year), there was not enough food to sustain anyone for long in any one place, and never enough to sustain a large group of people at a time. The Indians structured their communities accordingly. For most of the year, they followed the game animals in small, independent hunting

The traditional homelands of the various groups of subarctic Indians total some two million square miles, stretching across northern latitudes of North America from the Atlantic to the Pacific Ocean. The dotted lines show the modern boundaries of the Canadian provinces and the state of Alaska. The Beothuk of Newfoundland island became extinct in the early 1800s.

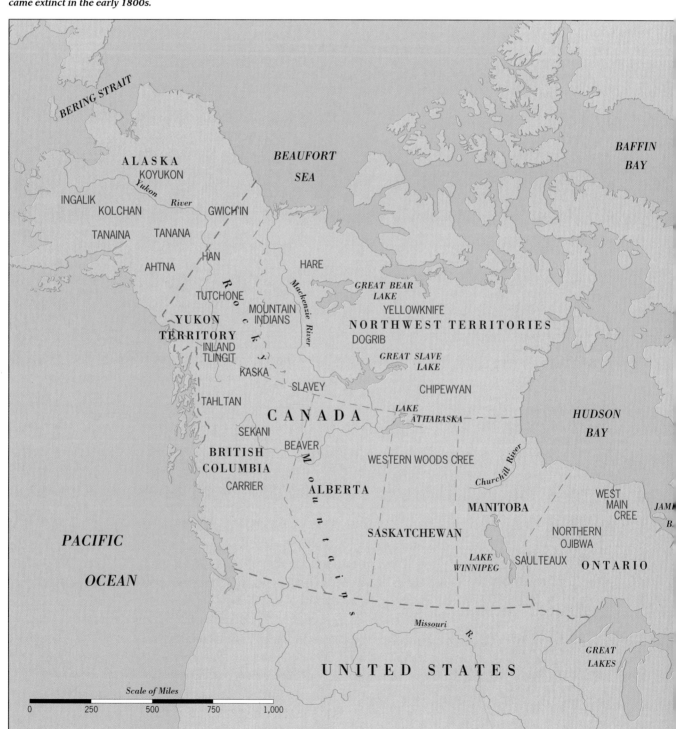

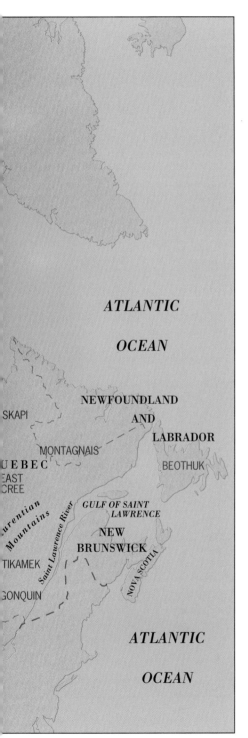

ATLANTIC

OCEAN

SKAPI

NEWFOUNDLAND

AND

LABRADOR

MONTAGNAIS

UEBEC

EAST
CREE

BEOTHUK

Laurentian
Mountains

GULF OF SAINT
LAWRENCE

Saint Lawrence River

NEW
BRUNSWICK

TIKAMEK

NOVA SCOTIA

GONQUIN

ATLANTIC

OCEAN

bands made up of a few families that were loosely led by a skilled hunter. Where they summered along lakes and rivers, they aggregated into larger bands, sometimes several hundred strong, composed of many related families or larger kinship groupings.

Since ancient times, the widely distributed population has been divided into two distinct linguistic stocks—Algonquian and Athapaskan. The Churchill River, which flows northeastward from Saskatchewan through northern Manitoba and into Hudson Bay, serves as a rough dividing line between the two language families. West of the river lie the traditional homelands of the Athapaskan speakers, including the Chipewyan, Beaver, Carrier, Sekani, Slavey, Dogrib, Yellowknife, Han, Hare, Kutchin (or Gwich'in, as they are called today), Ahtna, Tanana, Koyukon, and Ingalik. The Algonquian speakers, with the exception of some Western Woods Crees, live east of the Churchill. They include the West Main Cree, in the region south of Hudson Bay, and their neighbors to the immediate south, the Northern Ojibwa; the East Cree on the eastern side of James Bay; and the Montagnais and Naskapi of present-day Quebec and Labrador. Another Algonquian group, the Beothuk of the Island of Newfoundland, disappeared as an independent group in the early 19th century. A few Beothuks may have survived by joining Naskapi bands on the mainland; others died of disease or starvation, probably as a result of being cut off from their summertime coastal fish and game resources by the arrival of English settlers.

A distinct subarctic group came into being in the 1700s after generations of intermarriage between the white fur traders and Indian women. These were the Métis (a derivative of the French word for "mixed"), whose unique lifestyle combines elements of both the white and the Indian worlds. The majority of Métis are French-Cree, although there are many other combinations including Scottish-Cree, English-Cree, and some with blood ties to other subarctic groups. Most Métis speak an Algonquian dialect and either French, English, or both.

The modern tribal names assigned by the European newcomers differ from the names the Indians call themselves in their own languages. The Northern Ojibwa, for example, have never identified themselves as a tribal unit. Each band has always had its own name, usually associated either with a hunting ground or with the leader of the principal band family. The same holds for the Cree, who generally identify themselves as Cree only when they are speaking English or French. Otherwise, they use their band name. The generic name Cree was taken from a band of Indians who

NASKAPI WOMAN

hunted south of James Bay during the mid-17th century and called themselves Kenistenoag. The French recorded the name as Kristinaux and later shortened it to Kris, which eventually became Cree. In fact, the French did much to stamp the modern identities of several other groups of Indians. They dubbed a band of the Gwich'in people in central Alaska *les gens de large*—meaning "bands at large." The name has survived in English as Chandalar Gwich'in. Early French explorers also named the Montagnais. The word means "mountaineer" in French. The explorers chose it because the territory of those Indians was dominated by the Laurentian Mountains that parallel the Saint Lawrence River. Today many Montagnais and their neighboring kinsmen, the Naskapi, call themselves Innu, an Algonquian word meaning "people" or "human beings." The Cree also use variants of this same word to refer to native speakers of their language. Derived from a common root, its pronunciation varies from group to group. Similarly, many modern Athapaskans identify themselves as Dene, an Athapaskan term with a related meaning.

One of the first Europeans to study the language of the Montagnais was Father Paul Le Jeune, who arrived in Quebec in 1632 to take up the duties of superior of a band of Jesuits intent on converting the Algonquian speakers of the Saint Lawrence River valley. The French missionary found the tongue wanting "words for piety, devotion, virtue," but he also noted it was impossibly rich in other respects. Le Jeune described the language as having an infinite number of proper nouns, which could be translated into French only by circumlocutions. "They have so tiresome an abundance," lamented the priest, "that I am almost led to believe that I shall remain poor all my life in their language."

Le Jeune's observations reflected his own parochial viewpoint more than actual facts. Modern linguistic research has long since assembled overwhelming evidence that all aboriginal peoples, including speakers of the Algonquian and Athapaskan tongues, possess the linguistic ability to express both abstract and concrete thought, especially those ideas that are related to their own conceptions of the spiritual existence.

Language aside, the basic pattern of the subarctic way of life was similar from one end of the continent to the other. The legends of the

GWICH'IN WOMAN AND BABY

NASKAPI MAN

Algonquian-speaking Montagnais, for example, echo 3,000 miles away in the tales told by the Athapaskan-speaking Gwich'in. The rites of passage for young males, as well as those prescribed for females at menarche, also were comparable, and everywhere there was an openhanded generosity with food, even in bad times, that reflected the fundamental Indian ethic that the resources belong to everyone. Some bands adopted the ways of contiguous tribes—the Ingalik of western Alaska and the Tahltan of British Columbia, for instance, shared many cultural features with the neighboring Indians of the Pacific Northwest.

The forest and its animals provided all subarctic groups with the raw materials for tools, clothing, weaponry, and dwellings. While the majority of Algonquians used stone implements, the Athapaskans generally made their utensils out of either wood or animal products, such as bones, antlers, beaver teeth, or birds' beaks. Containers were generally fashioned from bark and made watertight with pitch. Although styles differed depending on the type of snow most frequently encountered, almost all snowshoes worn by subarctic peoples were made from a bent wooden frame with a rawhide webbing. They pulled their loads on toboggans (an Algonquian word for "sled") of bark, wood, or hide. The Indians also used the birch-bark canoe to navigate the numerous waterways. Both men and women wore buckskin shirts of varying lengths along with leggings that were attached to fur-lined moccasins. In cold weather, they added robes,

TAHLTAN COUPLE

CREE MAN

mittens, and caps made from the skins of hare, fox, muskrat, beaver, and mink. In summer, the subarctic peoples covered their bodies as protection against swarms of biting insects.

The most common type of housing was the portable, cone-shaped lodge, supported by light poles and covered with animal skins, tree boughs, or pieces of bark sewn together into mats. Some groups also built domed lodges with frameworks of bent saplings that were tied together at the top. Moss, mud, snow, and brush provided insulation. Bedding consisted of furred hides spread over a ground covering of freshly cut spruce boughs. When weather permitted, many Indians lived in simple lean-tos. A few groups constructed durable winter homes made of logs or planks.

No one knows quite how humans came to take up residence in the boreal forest. Although subarctic oral histories claim the people have always hunted their ancestral territories, modern scholars believe the subarctic Indians, like other Native Americans, came from Asia, some by boat, but most across the land bridge that spanned what is now the Bering Strait and linked Siberia and Alaska from about 25,000 to 10,000 years ago. The hunters would have followed the game herds, the bison and mammoth, caribou and muskoxen, drifting east into a world not yet inhabited by their kind. No doubt they would have been highly adapted to subarctic survival even then, trained in the taiga and tundra of Ice Age Siberia.

CREE GIRL

NASKAPI CHILDREN

Once in the New World, the paleo-hunters would have found a land that was largely sealed in glacial ice. To the east, the vast Laurentian ice sheet covered two-thirds of North America from south of the Great Lakes to the Arctic, and from the Saint Lawrence River to the eastern slopes of the northern Rockies. There the glaciers stopped, forming a narrow, ice-free corridor from Alaska to the American high plains; to the west, the coastal highlands were interred in ice from what is now Oregon to the Aleutian Islands. The subarctic peoples likely followed that corridor south, trailing the herds that fed them.

This first pulse of humans probably ventured out of Asia in small increments, perhaps hunting band by hunting band, gradually accumulating on the unpopulated continent. Some may have stayed in the North. But others continued into the southern forests and Great Plains, and some of these turned eastward, following the southern rim of glacial ice and the herds that grazed there. Their migration apparently occurred over millennia, steered by the gradual warming of the climate and the retreat of the Canadian ice sheets that began some 8,000 years ago. As the region hidden beneath the Laurentian ice became accessible to them, the Proto-Algonquians moved northward into that new land, drawn by its immense herds of caribou.

Meanwhile, a second group entered the hemisphere from the west, bringing with them a distinctively Eurasian technology—the small, double-

NASKAPI MAN

WOMAN, PROBABLY SLAVEY OR DOGRIB

edged, razor-sharp stone chips called microblades. This group evidently crossed just before the land bridge vanished into the rising sea level of a warmer climate; their faint trail of artifacts places them in Alaska about 11,000 years ago. It is likely that these relative newcomers from Asia became the Athapaskan speakers of more recent times—perhaps the ancestors of the Gwich'in, whose 1,000-year-old artifacts have been found at a site near Klo-Kut in the northern Yukon Territory, or the Chipewyan and Yellowknife bands, that stalked the caribou north of Great Slave Lake in the present-day Northwest Territories 2,000 years ago.

Not until about 2500 BC, when the ice had retreated back to the tundra, did the present boreal forest begin to cover the continent. Then, as the roving bands moved into the stands of spruce and fir, their lives settled into the rhythms that endured more or less intact for some 30 centuries—until the arrival of the Europeans. Little changed during those millennia; a hard winter in 2000 BC was much like a hard winter in AD 1500.

That ageless way of life was defined and sustained—often marginally—by a land like no other. Its main feature is the Canadian Shield, a 1.6-million-square-mile slab of granite and gneiss laid down in a rough U shape in which Hudson Bay forms the open center. The grinding of glacial ice and its abrasive load of gravel and sand polished away the soil in some areas, exposing the underlying granite as ridges and cliffs. Elsewhere the glaciers pushed layers of clay, sand, and gravel across the shield, etching the complex filigree of terrain that, filled with water, became a wonderland of rivers and lakes, many of them virtual inland seas. On its Atlantic side, the shield has been wrinkled into mountains and ridges, worn down to geological stumps by ice and weather. West of Hudson Bay, the shield ends where its exposed flank was notched with huge lakes—Great Bear, Athabaska, and Great Slave, the source of the Mackenzie River. Over all of this lies a dense pelt of spruce, fir, and pine, interspersed with groves of birch, aspen, and willow—a covering that thins with latitude, eventually giving way to the eternally frozen land beyond the timberline. Lowlands offer a counterpoint. Along the southern margins of Hudson and James Bays, the sharply defined lakes and tributary rivers of the shield give way to marshes and muskegs, as the Indians call peat bogs.

West of the Mackenzie River, which flows from Great Slave Lake through a northward-tapering valley to empty into the Arctic's Beaufort Sea, the earth's crust has been tortured into parallel ranges of mountains, from the Rockies to the Pacific, and the land, still swathed in dark forests, acquires a daunting complexity. In this mountainous realm, the defining river is the Yukon, which begins its meandering journey in British Columbia, then snakes its way north and west across Canada's Yukon Territory and central Alaska, bound for the Bering Sea. Those features—of plateau and lowland, of river and mountain—define not only the terrain but also how life must be lived there.

It is an inhospitable domain to strangers, where winters are deep, dark, and long, with temperatures plunging far below freezing for months at a time. Summers are short and warm, but in some ways even less tolerable. Voracious mosquitoes hatch by the millions as soon as the snows begin to melt, to be replaced by clouds of black flies. There is the illusion of fecundity; although the boreal forest teems with wildlife, its resources are widely distributed, always uncertain, always on the move. For prey and predator alike, the land delivers good times and bad, feast and famine, life and death, on a schedule no one can fully know.

The principal game animals were the caribou and the moose, which provided meat for food; skins and sinews for clothing, snowshoes, and shelter; and bone for weapons and tools. The people on the northern edge of the region hunted the so-called Barren Ground caribou, which migrated annually in vast numbers from the open crown forests to tundra and back again, feeding largely on moss. Out on the tundra, migrating herds could be killed in great numbers using a weirlike fence of spruce that funneled the animals into a surround, where the hunters finished them off with lances and spears. In the woodlands to the south, the dense foliage prevents moss from covering the ground, precluding the caribou but providing a lush supply of tree and shrub twigs for moose. The Indians hunted moose from canoes and on foot during the summer; in winter, they sought them in the deep snow of the forest, or in the yards, or clearings, of trampled snow where several of the big, solitary animals tended to gather. Within this closed crown forest region are areas of hilly or rocky land where moss grows in sufficient quantities to support small groups of caribou. Hunters often drove these woodland caribou into the water where an archer in a birch-bark canoe could overhaul the swimming animals and kill them. The smaller creatures—beaver, porcupine, hare, and the migratory water birds—were taken with traps, snares, and bow and arrows. In the mountains, the hunters went after mountain goats. The black bear was also hunted, usually by coaxing the creature out of the deep sleep of hibernation with gentle exhortations and false calls of

A 19th-century painting of a Montagnais lodge in eastern Canada shows the conical frame of slender poles lined with bark or hides; this style was easy to transport and erect. An overturned canoe sits by the side of the dwelling.

Montagnais Lodge at Mingan.

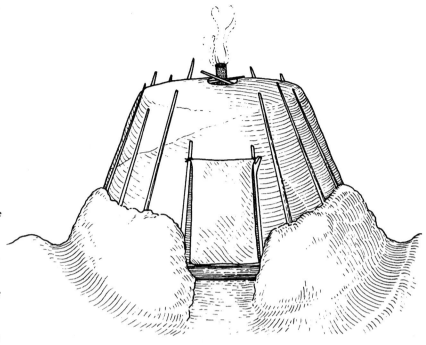

The dome-shaped lodge, favored by the Naskapi, features stakes driven into the ground and covered with bark, canvas, or hides. Piled snow provides insulation. "Such a lodge when the icy wind beats on the walls outside is a very snug place," wrote a white observer.

carrion-eating birds. Fish from the numerous lakes and rivers were staples almost everywhere. Plants and berries provided variety and often in lean times were foods of last resort.

During the 1630s, the Jesuit Paul Le Jeune observed the Indian ways of subsistence, and reflected on how their daily habits might impinge on his plans for them. As he was ignorant of how the Montagnais planned their yearly harvesting of game animals, it seemed to him that the souls of the Indians could be saved only if they settled into an agrarian life. "Not much ought to be hoped for from the savages," he wrote, "as long as they are wanderers; you will instruct them today, tomorrow hunger snatches your hearers away, forcing them to go and seek their food in the rivers and woods." These hunters did not live from harvest to harvest, as farmers do, but from day to day, hour to hour, meal to meal.

"Their only thought is to live," observed Le Jeune. "These people do not think there is any other science in the world except that of eating and drinking; and in this lies all their philosophy. They are astonished at the value we place upon books, seeing that a knowledge of them does not give us anything with which to drive away hunger. They cannot understand what we ask from God in our prayers. 'Ask him,' they say to me, 'for moose, bears, and beavers; tell him that thou wishest them to eat'; and when I tell them that those are only trifling things, that there are still greater riches to demand, they laughingly reply, 'What couldst thou wish better than to eat thy fill of these good dishes?' In short, they have nothing but life; yet they are not always sure of that, since they often die of hunger."

The Montagnais response to the Black Robes, as the Indians called the priests, was in fact utterly logical. The Indians often judged their own shamans, or holy men, as powerful on the basis of their ability to predict,

A Cree winter lodge made of logs (above) can hold up to four families, each with its own corner of the cabin. Women are responsible for carpeting the floor with spruce boughs (right), which they replenish two to three times each week to keep the dwelling warm and fresh smelling.

A Cree infant takes her first tentative steps, an occasion for celebration in her community. She walks across spruce boughs to signify the role she will later have in gathering branches to cover the floor of her home.

or even bring about, bountiful harvests of game animals, and were probably applying the same standards to the Jesuits.

In the fall of 1632, Le Jeune attempted to winter with a band of Montagnais, but quickly gave it up as too strenuous an undertaking. The priest was in no condition to match the Indians' pace. "I do not believe that, out of 100 clerics, there would be 10 who could endure the hardships to be encountered in following them," he later noted.

Le Jeune would soon discover that life in the subarctic was keyed to the freezing point of water. When it was unfrozen, water offered a network of lakes and tributaries, so that a canoe could travel many miles without more than a short portage. These were the more or less settled times, the summers when relatively large groups of Indians converged in the bug-free breezes off a lake or river and subsisted on local game, fish, and berries, moving easily by canoe. Summers meant the renewal of kinship bonds and the warmth of socialization, a time when many hunting bands mingled and intermarried.

The worst times were the intervals of transition, when water was in the process of freezing or melting. A delayed spring breakup of ice on lakes and rivers would keep the people penned up, unable to use their canoes. An early breakup would whirl into a flood. A freeze that came too

A glimpse into the interior (above) of a tent pitched in the Mackenzie River region shows a mother and child eating, while a baby sleeps in an overhead cradle. In the photograph at right, a Chipewyan family gathers outside its summer tent, set up in a pleasant glade of aspens. Once fashioned from caribou hide, these shelters in modern times are customarily made of canvas.

A Slavey winter house measures about 20 feet across the front and 10 feet along the sides. The rectangular opening at the top allows smoke to escape; mud, moss, and brush are caked between the logs to block icy winds and blowing snow.

early could rime the waters with enough ice to impede canoeing, but not enough to walk on, isolating the hunters from the game animals. Too much moisture turned their world into a trackless bog. Too little snow made hunting impossible; too much masked the vital chronicle of tracks and sign.

With the coming of winter and a hard freeze across the land, the people dispersed in small bands. Hunting became easier, and the frozen lakes and rivers transformed into highways of ice. Then hunters could get out on their snowshoes—Le Jeune called them *raquettes*—and fairly fly along the hard crust covering the drifts. Then it became possible to hunt the woodland caribou, the moose, the black bear, and the beaver holed up in their lodges. Hard winters with deep, ice-crusted snow and good hunting—those were the best of times. Yet winter was also the period of intense isolation for most groups, when there was no contact with others. Too much isolation was dangerous, for it sometimes drove people insane. And when game was lacking, winter was also the time of famine and starvation. Among the Algonquians, winter was the season of Windigo; among the Athapaskans, of the Nakani, a similar bogeyman.

In 1633 Le Jeune made a second attempt to winter with the Montagnais, finding another host who was willing to take a Black Robe. From that often harrowing experience, he drew a detailed account of Indian life in the areas around the small French settlements.

On October 18, Le Jeune embarked with the Montagnais aboard a small flotilla of canoes and heavier, masted vessels. The band sailed for nearly a month down the Saint Lawrence River, stopping to hunt among the numerous islands that they came across during their journey. For a time, the priest reported, the Indians enjoyed one feast after another. Other Montagnais joined the group. On November 12, the Indians left their boats and some of their baggage and headed into the forest. The band consisted of three families, with 45 people in all—19 in Le Jeune's group, 16 in a second, and 10 in a third. Once camped, the hunters searched for signs of game. They stayed in that camp until the game was hunted or frightened away, then they struck off for another.

"They begin by having breakfast," Le Jeune reported, "if there is any; for sometimes they depart without breakfasting, continue on their way without dining, and go to bed without supping." The women would strike

A Tutchone group in the Yukon Territory stands in front of a typical plank house. Although the Tutchone traditionally had favored conical lodges or domed tents, they began to build wooden homes in the style of their Northwest Coast neighbors about the turn of the 20th century.

the lodge, shaking off its ice and snow and stowing the poles and the bark covering, which they packed on their backs in long bundles that were held with a cord across their foreheads. "When everyone is loaded," wrote the priest, "they mount their snowshoes, which are bound to the feet so that they will not sink into the snow, and then they march over plain and mountain, making the little ones go on ahead, who start early, and often do not arrive until quite late. These little ones have their load, or sledge, to accustom them early to fatigue; and they try to stimulate them to see who will carry or drag the most."

Once they were under way, the going was hard. "If it happened to thaw, Oh God, what suffering!" observed the priest. "It seemed to me I was walking over a road of glass, which broke under my feet at every step. The frozen snow, beginning to melt, would fall and break into blocks or big pieces, into which we often sank up to our knees, and, sometimes, to our waists. If there was pain in falling, there was still more in pulling ourselves out, for our raquettes were loaded with snow, and became so heavy that, when we tried to draw them out, it seemed as if somebody were tugging at our legs to dismember us."

Le Jeune remembered the Montagnais pole-and-bark shelters as cramped and dismal affairs. The floor was a several-foot-deep ring or square cleared in the snow, then carpeted with fir branches. At one end, facing the southeastern dawn, a rough entry was cut in the snow, its door an animal skin. "You cannot stand upright in this house," Le Jeune wrote, "as much on account of its low roof as the suffocating smoke; and conse-

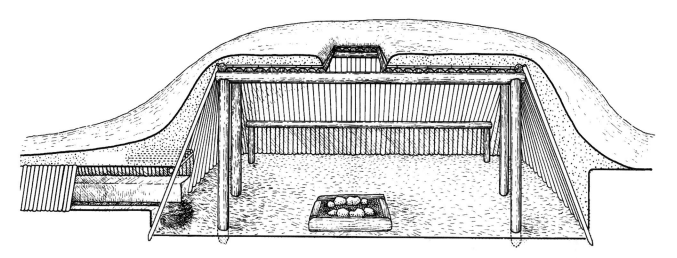

The Koyukon of the Koyukuk River basin in central Alaska built dugout dwellings covered with an insulating layer of earth, similar in style to the homes of their Eskimo trading partners. The narrow entrance tunnel (shown on the left) was designed to block icy drafts.

quently you must always lie down, or sit flat upon the ground. When you go out, the cold, the snow, and the danger of getting lost in these great woods drive you in again more quickly than the wind, and keep you a prisoner in a dungeon which has neither lock nor key."

Inside the lodge there was no room to maneuver. "You cannot move to right or left, for your neighbors are at your elbows; you cannot withdraw to the rear, for you encounter the wall of snow, or the bark of the cabin which shuts you in." Where heat from the fire melted the snow wall, the water swiftly turned to ice. But the broiling heat on one side, and the freezing cold on the other, were not the worst of it. The smoke, declared Le Jeune, "is martyrdom. It almost killed me and made me weep continually, although I had neither grief nor sadness in my heart. It sometimes grounded all of us who were in the cabin; that is, it caused us to place our mouths against the earth in order to breathe. For, although the savages were accustomed to this torment, yet occasionally it became so dense that they, as well as I, were compelled to prostrate themselves, and as it were to eat the earth, so as not to drink the smoke. I have sometimes remained several hours in this position, especially during the most severe cold and when it snowed; for it was then the smoke assailed us with the greatest fury." The cold outside was so intense, Le Jeune reported, that tree trunks burst with a cannonlike report.

And there were the dogs. At the time of Le Jeune's wintering with the Montagnais, small dogs were the only animal domesticated by the subarctic Indians, who used them mainly as pack animals and for hunting; their role as sled pullers came later. The dogs enjoyed a degree of protection without much respect.

"These animals," Le Jeune wrote, "being famished, as they have nothing to eat, any more than we, do nothing but run to and fro gnawing at

Wielding bow saws, two teams of Trout Lake woodcutters (left) work from opposite sides of a log. The team that saws through the log first wins.

Competitors in the tea boiling contest (below) must cut up kindling, arrange a campfire, light it with a match and paper, and heat a pot of water and tea until the mixture boils.

Young men beating caribou-hide drums (right) accompany the Drum Dance, in which the entire community participates.

FESTIVALS TO REKINDLE A RICH HERITAGE

Until well into the 20th century, the Dene of the Great Slave Lake region of northwest Canada lived largely as they always had. Although Christian missionaries had altered the age-old Dene custom of gathering at the lakeshore in summer by promoting Christmas and Easter get-togethers at the trading post and mission settlements, and fur traders had introduced metal tools, firearms, and new foods such as tea, rice, and flour, the Indians still relied largely on their hunting, gathering, and fishing skills for their subsistence.

After World War II, however, the lives of the Dene changed dramatically. While programs introduced by the Canadian government, such as compulsory education, medical services, and welfare payments, improved economic and social conditions in some instances, they also weakened traditional leadership and threatened traditional Dene values.

Despite these pressures, the Dene have found ways, like the Slavey winter festival at Trout Lake pictured here, to preserve and promote their rich heritage and cultural identity. Usually held in early March when the worst of the winter cold is over, these festivals bring together hundreds of families for many days of celebration, much like the gatherings of old. Activities requiring traditional skills, such as snowshoe racing for children and adults, dogsledding, log cutting, tea boiling, moose calling, hand games, storytelling, singing, drum dancing, and feasting, help the Dene rekindle old friendships, make new friends, and reestablish their community.

Taking an overlong stride lands a snow-shoe racer in trouble (right), to the amusement of his friends.

everything in the cabin. Now as we were as often lying down as sitting up in these bark houses, they frequently walked over our faces and stomachs; and so often and persistently, that, being tired of shouting at them and driving them away, I would sometimes cover my face and then give them liberty to go where they wanted."

In better times, when Le Jeune tossed a bit of meat to the dogs, "the savages began to suspect something, from the fight that afterwards took place among those animals, and commenced to cry out against me, saying that I was contaminating their feast, that they would capture nothing more, and that we would die of hunger." Le Jeune was ignorant of the Montagnais custom regarding proper respect for the flesh and bones of game animals. After his unwitting blunder, he sensed that the women and children of the group looked upon him with more than their usual disdain—they habitually chided him with such insults as, "He is captain of the dogs"—and said he would be the cause of their death.

In fact, Le Jeune found their situation to be precarious. They were wintering on the west side of the Saint Lawrence, at that time choked with ice floes. The hunting was not good—shallow snow meant big game could not be taken. The men brought home nothing but beaver and porcupine, "but in so small a number and so seldom that they kept us from dying

Harnessed sled dogs wearing beaded blankets rest outside a cabin in the Yukon Territory. Essential to Indian transport since the arrival of the Europeans, the dogs often have been adorned with a variety of decorations.

rather than helped us to live." Toward the end of their food supply, Le Jeune said that with "the skin of an eel for my day's fare, I considered that I had breakfasted, dined, and supped well."

It was not long before the Jesuit and his hosts were reduced to gnawing on old moose hides and branches. People from other bands came to their lodge with reports that their companions had starved to death. "I saw some who had eaten only once in five days, and considered themselves very well off if they found something to dine upon at the end of two days; they were reduced to skeletons, being little more than skin and bones." When one of their own number was dying of hunger, Le Jeune noted, the others drifted toward despair.

The Jesuit returned to the French settlement at Trois Rivières in April. He had lived at 23 different camps in six months, surviving weeks of famine and once being lost in the woods. Despite his proximity to his hosts, however, Le Jeune had experienced only the physical reality of the northland; his Roman Catholic faith blinded him to the mental reality—to the spirits that have always been as pervasive a part of life as hunger.

"It is as though one were to walk through a field of tall grass, and suddenly discover that his eyes had deceived him, that each blade waving in the wind was a snake," wrote Cornelius Osgood, a Yale University ethnographer who lived among Alaska's Peel River Gwich'in in the early 1930s. Osgood was describing the animate world of one Athapaskan-speaking band, but his subject could have been the world-view of any subarctic people. The uncertainty of life produced a close kinship between individuals and their surroundings. The northern world was everywhere alive, inhabited by animate rocks and waters, winds and sky, animal spirits and souls of the dead, giants and monsters.

"The Indians believed that a stump could momentarily change to a man, that the caribou could push back the hood from its face and gaze out of a human countenance, that the snake or the owl could address the sleeping Indian in his own tongue," noted Diamond Jenness, a Canadian who spent decades studying the lifeways of various subarctic groups. Yet this universe was the subject of a complex mingling of respect, love, gratitude, and fear; humans

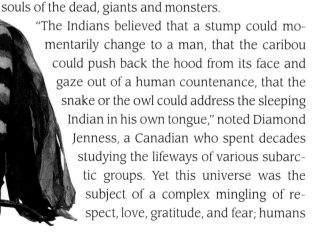

The Métis adorned their sled dogs' harnesses with ornaments called standing irons. One Hudson's Bay Company wife recalled guests arriving for a New Year's celebration: "Several miles away from the fort, they made a stop to smarten themselves and the dogs. Foxtails and colored ribbons decorated the leather collars and standing irons."

Intricately painted motifs adorn a Naskapi hunter's caribou-skin coat. Every coat of this type bore a unique design inspired by a dream. The hunter's wife interpreted the message into designs that she painted on the coat.

inhabited it without being its master. The world of the forest contained power higher than that of the humans who struggled there. To the Algonquians, that higher power was invested in spirits called manitous, but all of the hunting bands recognized some sort of supernatural beings and accommodated them in similar ways.

Consequently, such universally prized substances as tobacco were thrown on the fire, or a pile of sticks accumulated in a sacred place. Some Algonquian-speaking groups sacrificed a white dog to appeal to good spirits and deflect approaching evil ones. Prayers urged bad spirits to go away and torment one's enemies, while favor was curried with good spirits by offering feathers and sweet grasses and fir branches. Many rituals had to do with controlling the weather. People prayed for deeper snow or, if the snow was already deep, for an end to the blizzard that wiped away the tracks of game. If there was a thaw, they prayed for a hard freeze. The Montagnais tossed scarce grease on the campfire and expressed their needs in this succinct prayer: "Make us find something to eat."

Access to the world of spirits was gained through vision quests, the vehicle of enlightenment for adolescent boys—and sometimes for girls— who were made to endure days of privation under the strict control of adults. The goal was to acquire a guardian spirit, often an animal, who would invest the quester with its power. The experience of gaining a spirit helper filled the Indians with awe, and few dared to reveal their visions for fear of offending the spirit and forfeiting its blessing.

Occasionally the supernatural contact left some physical remnant for the quester to use as an amulet. More often, people subsequently made or found some object that figured in their dream. One Algonquian-speaking Indian described by Jenness had preserved a hair. It was pulled from the mustache of a manitou, the Indian claimed, adding that "I would have been drowned a hundred times had it not been for this hair. It is this which has enabled me to kill moose, has preserved me from sickness, and has made me live so long. I have cured the sick with this hair; there is nothing that I cannot do with it."

But the power of amulets was relative. If the guardian spirit failed, the amulet was discarded. Moreover, the power could be neither inherited nor transferred to others. And not everyone received the gift. After an unsuccessful vision quest, one dejected Athapaskan boy reportedly lamented, "Nothing saw me, nothing wanted me."

Dreams were a portal to the spirit world. "They have," wrote Father Le Jeune, "great faith in their dreams, imagining that what they have seen in their sleep must happen, and that they must execute whatever they have thus imagined. This is a great misfortune, for if a savage dreams that he will die if he does not kill me, he will take my life the first time he meets me alone. Our savages ask almost every morning, 'Hast thou not seen any beavers or moose, while sleeping?' " To dream of animals meant that one was going to hunt them successfully. They were dreams of food.

In every group of Native Americans there were men—and occasionally women—who possessed extraordinary skill in hunting, gambling, or healing. They seemed to their fellow Indians to have a special influence with the world of spirits. These people were the shamans. Some Northern Ojibwa shamans coalesced into the fraternity of Midewiwin, a priesthood especially associated with botanical medicines, that orchestrated seasonal initiations, divinations, and other rites, acting as interlocutors between the spheres of spirits and humans.

A shaman's gatekeeping status was reinforced by demonstrations of special powers. In the shaking tent ceremony of the Northern Ojibwa and Cree, for example, a shaman entered a small hide enclosure, which began to tremble as the manitous and other spirits entered. Their voices could sometimes be heard squeaking from the tent or speaking in conventional tones. For people with little time for ceremony, the shaking tent was both a spiritual event and welcome entertainment. Not that the rite was viewed frivolously—one shaman told a white observer in the 1930s that his fear of entering the woods alone was a punishment for deceiving his people by shaking the tent himself.

Not all shamans were devoted to good works. Some used their powers to inflict pain and misfortune. An accusation of sorcery, if not denied, was enough to establish a shaman as a sorcerer. Among some groups, shamans had to keep their witchcraft activities secret or risk being killed. In others, the power to do evil was tolerable provided it was used in retaliation, but not if applied unprovoked.

But shamans were not needed for the day-to-day divination that marked the northern hunter's existence. That was a matter of reading an immense mnemonic catalog of subtle possibilities. Among the East Cree Mistassini band, anomalously shaped or sized objects were often used to predict the future. If a porcupine had an intestine with an unusual shape, for example, the hunter might give it to his wife or mother to make into a tiny container, which she filled with the melted fat from the intestines of the porcupine. The special feature of this sac was the shape of an appendage, and this shape told the hunter what game he could expect to kill. If the shape had a sharp angle, like the foreleg of a caribou, a caribou kill was predicted. If the angle was rounded, it meant a bear or an otter. An intermediate angle indicated a moose. Animal-shaped rocks, fish bones, lumps on beaver jawbones, certain bird calls, a special crackling sound from the fire—all were employed as tools of divination.

The Indians living in the North also were able to read the future in the fractures of charred scapulas, or shoulder bones. In the practice of this divination method, the level of difficulty increased with the size of the animal whose scapula was employed. Not everyone in the band possessed sufficient spiritual power to read the fire-induced cracks in a moose or caribou scapula, but smaller animals' scapulas were within the common grasp.

In the uncertain silences of the boreal forest, no less than in the parallel world of charms and spirits, humans were manifestly tiny, insular, and alone. Their creator, if indeed they believed in such a being, was beyond helping them. As Father Le Jeune recorded more than 300 years ago, the Montagnais spoke of Atachocam, who created the world, "as one speaks of a thing so far distant that nothing sure can be known about it." Although game belonged to everyone, in equal measure, animals—and, indeed, the world—belonged really to the hunter. His proficiency spelled the

SHAKEN BY THE SPIRITS

Conjuring—the invocation of spirits to seek guidance and direction—takes one of its most vivid forms in the ritual known as the shaking tent ceremony. Combining religious conviction and a reverence for animals, it is practiced in the same way by a good number of northern Indians, with small variations.

Most elements are universal: The shaking tent ceremony is always held after dark and always requires a barrel-shaped lodge built according to specific guidelines under the watchful eye of the conjurer—although he himself does not participate in the construction. It is in here that the conjurer kneels, calling on the spirits by praying, singing, and sometimes smoking a pipe.

As the spirits arrive, the tent shakes wildly, with the top sometimes tracing an arc of about three feet in diameter. For those sitting outside, the voices of the spirits themselves are heard coming from within—fish, turtles, or other animals, perhaps, or maybe Mista'peo, the chief spirit of many eastern Algonquian peoples. The spirits respond to a whole host of requests: to find a lost or missing relative; to determine why someone is sick (and what can be done about it); to predict the success of the hunt; and to see into the future. Despite the serious nature of the questions, the mood is not always somber. Sometimes people in the gathering call out to the spirits in funny voices (and the spirits reply in kind), and sometimes the spirits share jokes or puzzles with the group.

At the conclusion of the ceremony, the people leave quietly. The tent is immediately dismantled, and the poles and hoops are disposed of in a "clean" area. The sticks may never be used for anything else; indeed, it is said to be very bad luck if they are disturbed in any way.

An experienced builder tests the pliability of young evergreen trees before selecting the right ones for a shaking tent. Two trees will be bent into hoops and lashed to six nine-foot poles set in a circle four feet in diameter. Animal skins or canvas cover the tent, which is open at the top to let spirits come and go.

During the ceremony, men and women sit separately, several feet away from the shaking tent, eager to hear what the spirits have to say. The messages are often both prophetic and entertaining, as the spirits try to amuse or trick the listeners.

After the shaking tent ceremony, a young boy offers cigarettes to the conjurer. Tobacco pervades this ritual, as it does many others: An initial offering is smoked by the people gathered for the ceremony. Later, the spirits themselves sometimes request cigarettes, which are passed in to them in the tent by the people outside.

The conjurer's coveted ability to communicate with the spirits has typically come to him in a dream during puberty. Throughout the shaking tent ceremony, he kneels with his buttocks resting on his heels, bent over at the waist with his head nearly touching the ground. Afterward, all are honored with a feast or tobacco offering.

A Tahltan shaman (left, center) wearing a dancing shirt and Chilkat blanket stands with other dancers and children outside a wooden lodge in British Columbia.

difference between feast and famine, life and death; it also calibrated his access to the animal spirits. Among such men, the fragmented subarctic communities found their leaders.

A subarctic chief achieved influence among his people by virtue of his hunting prowess, wisdom, and relationship with the spirit world. If he was a war leader, he gained status by virtue of his fighting ability. Even then, he led at the pleasure of his comrades. The leader was first among equals. "They have reproached me a hundred times because we fear our captains," reported Le Jeune, "while they laugh at and make sport of theirs. All the authority of their chief is in his tongue's end, for he is powerful in so far as he is eloquent; and, even if he kills himself talking and haranguing, he will not be obeyed unless he pleases the savages."

The qualities the Indians valued most echo through their stories. Every group has tales of heroes who trick their way to success. Among the Gwich'in, for example, an elaborate set of cycles evolved that explained how the world and its creatures came to be the way they are. Raven, the quintessential trickster of many Indian tales, made dry land, stole the sun that

Shamans such as the Athapaskan man at right performed rituals to cure illnesses or to ensure a good hunt. Charlie Yahey (left), a dreamer, or prophet, of the Beaver people, displays the ceremonial drumhead painted by his spiritual mentor. It is based on a dream journey through the Beaver cosmos.

Bear kept in a sack by his bed, and, aided by Fox, freed the moon. But Raven was too deceitful for his own good—and, ultimately, no match for the human hunter who killed Raven for always warning game with his caws. The Gwich'in culture hero Jateaquoint traveled a picaresque road to discovery, employing duplicity and occasional murder to good effect. Such stories help explain how humans and animals came to their present accord. A long time ago, according to the Gwich'in, some animals had been man-eaters but were tamed into game by Jateaquoint, who taught even Black Bear not to eat humans. Indeed, the Han and Great Bear Lake people believed that animals had once been men, and the Dogrib, who believed humans were reincarnated as animals, thought wild creatures understood human speech.

Subarctic folklore resonates with the merging of humans and animals, and even of their intermarriage. The tales spread into a web of taboos, intended to avoid offending powerful spirits—especially those of game animals. The taboos varied slightly from group to group. Among the Gwich'in, for example, dog, wolf, fox, wolverine, raven, and eagle could not be eaten; the heads of game animals and bodies of fur animals could not be left where dogs might eat them; a hunter who counted dead animals after a kill would offend their spirits; smoke from caribou and moose bones burned on a fire would drive those animals away; trapped lynx and fox had to be strangled, not clubbed, while marten and rabbit were killed by pinching the heart; speaking badly of an animal made it less willing to accept being killed.

Cree tradition holds that the cycle of the hunt depends on an elaborate set of rules designed to show respect for the slain animal. Accordingly, the children are not allowed to run out to greet their hunter fathers. The Cree believe that game should first be shown to the old people in the band. It is not proper for a child—or a dog—to impede that first contact. The women of the camp cannot express excitement as the hunters return, and the men must reveal their catch modestly—even an unintentional boast may insult the animal spirits.

Nowhere was greater care taken not to offend than in the hunting of bear. According to the anthropologist Frank Speck, who conducted fieldwork among the Montagnais and East Cree from about 1910 to the 1930s, the black bear offered the closest thing the subarctic Indian knew of truly ceremonial religion. Various hunters told him that the bear occupied this

The caribou-hoof rattle (above) and the bait box made of bone (right) were practical tools used by subarctic hunters. The bait box held a paste made from beaver glands that was smeared on traps and snares to attract a variety of prey. The rattle was attached by a line to an underwater beaver net; when the animal moved against the net, the rattle signaled the hunter to haul the net shut.

exalted position because it looked and thought like a man. In those instances when the caribou formed a tribe ruled by an overlord, they said, every bear was himself a chief unto himself.

The hunters tracked a bear in autumn so that they could kill it later during hibernation. After the animal had entered its snow-covered den, they would gather near the air hole, stained yellow by the sleeping bear's breath, and call: "Come out, grandfather!" or, sometimes, "My grandfather, I will light your pipe!" or "Come out, grandfather, already the sun is warm enough for you to come forth. Show me your head, grandfather." When the drowsy animal stumbled into the light, the hunters would kill him with a club, then gather for a smoke, being careful to put a bit of tobacco in their victim's mouth as well.

Ka'kwa, a venerable shaman of the East Cree Mistassini band, described the bear ritual in 1915, being careful not to use the animal's real name. "When they kill 'Short Tail,'" he recounted, "before they bring him in, the young unmarried women cover their faces. This is done so that they may not see the 'Great Food' coming in, lest they become sick on account of having insulted him. Only the married women may skin him, and only the men can cut him up. Then only the oldest men can eat his head. The tail must not be severed lest he be insulted. The right arm is cooked beside the fire. It must not be cut from the paw. Only the oldest man in the camp may eat it." Only the men could eat the heart and pick at the leg bones, which would cause a woman to be crippled by sore legs. The fried guts and grease were thrown into the fire, as an offering to Mista'peo, the soul-spirit of every Cree. "The 'Great Food' must not be eaten out of doors for it would be improper. It must not even be chewed outside the tent by the children, as this would be improper in respect to the 'Great Food.'"

The skull had to be picked clean and carried through the winter, then, in the late spring, raised on a tall pole at the gathering place. Tobacco was put in the animal's nose, and his chin and lower lip were cleaned and decorated with beads "so that the 'One Who Owns the Chin' will be satisfied."

In the northland, however, even taboos had to hold some practical value. Designed to ward off bad luck, taboos could be abandoned when misfortune struck. But taboos also cut two ways. A Cree hunter, for example, might fashion a hare out of snow and set it facing north, the domain of the spirit Ciiwetinsuu, who controlled the winter weather. Insulted, Ciiwetinsuu would send a storm to punish the hunter—at a time when colder weather was just what the hunter needed most. A clever person could thus invert taboos, transforming punishments into rewards.

The hunt was the men's domain, like the fashioning of tools and weapons and the building of sleds, like the important readings of prophecy from fractures in a charred shoulder bone. Women, it could be fairly said, did everything else, including adding finishing touches to some of the manufactured items, such as lacing the snowshoe frames made by the men. While the men sought large game, women snared the rabbits and birds that often kept the band alive between major kills. When the men returned to camp with a moose or caribou, the women turned the animal into pemmican, dried meat, and other food; women tanned hides, and manufactured and repaired clothing, moccasins, and mittens. Women picked berries in summer and did most of the fishing, along with the arduous work of cutting and drying fish for winter, which was never very far away.

Subarctic women worked hard to keep their camps clean and warm, and were highly creative cooks, capable of fixing a variety of tasty meals. To an outside observer, the women's lives may have seemed worse than they really were. Certainly, their lives were appalling to some European eyes. "The women do all the drudgery in winter, collect firewood, haul the sleighs along with the dogs, bring snow for water," wrote one visitor to the Han. "The women are not allowed to eat until their husbands are satisfied. They treat their wives generally with kindness, but are very jealous of them." Another explorer, writing in the 18th century, noted that women did all the heavy work and hauled the heaviest loads. Their husbands could beat or kill them with impunity—and even use them as gambling stakes.

In every subarctic band, the advent of female puberty, as evidenced by the onset of menstruation, was attended by an elaborate convergence of taboos. The spirit power of women, it was believed, was particularly strong during these times; their condition endangered the band because it could drive away fish and game. Thus the menarche was the most demanding of a lifetime's avoidances, especially among the Athapaskan speakers. The Han, for example, celebrated the event with a feast something like that prepared to mark a boy's first kill. After the feast, however, the girl was sent to live in isolation for a year under the care of a relative of her future husband. They camped in a separate shelter, where the girl lived on fish, berries, and caribou soup. She could drink water only through a tube and was forbidden to eat fresh meat—to do so would have spoiled the hunting for the following year.

When the girl walked abroad, she donned a full-length hood that forced her to watch the ground at her feet—she could not look at men—

Mountain Indians build a moose-skin boat for use on the Keele River in the Mackenzie Mountains. An observer of one of the boats described it as "eight or 10 skins sewn together, with the seams sealed with hard grease stretched over a framework of green pliable poles."

and she could not follow an established trail, as that would bring bad luck to a hunter. If she had to travel, her husband-to-be towed her with a six-foot pole or she went in her own boat; anyone walking in the tracks of such a woman would develop sore legs. The commemoration of menarche varied in detail from group to group—among the Slavey, for example, seclusion lasted only 10 days, and a month among the Upper Tanana. Afterward the woman went into seclusion only during menstruation, in a monthly ritual that lasted until menopause.

Constrained though her life was in such respects, an Indian woman was not without influence. To the horror of the Jesuit Le Jeune, Montagnais women were allowed to actively court the men they favored, divorce at will, and take lovers in addition to their husbands. They also steered the band's important decisions. "The choice of plans, of undertak-

Only females are permitted to gather around a Slavey girl at the time of her menstrual period. During such seclusions, a Tahltan girl wore a bag (inset) containing animal grease, which she smeared on her lips to curb her appetite.

ings, of journeys, of winterings, lies in nearly every instance in the hands of the housewife," Le Jeune noted. The men were concerned with the tactical business of the hunt. Women were the band's administrators and the men's hardworking partners.

Husbands came from outside the hunting band, but usually not from very far outside—even the summer gatherings were not large enough to supply many strangers. Thus, from Labrador to Alaska, pairings generally linked cousins, with minor variations on that theme. Among the Han, for example, the preferred marriage was between a man and his mother's brother's daughter—what anthropologists call a cross-cousin match. The Slavey preferred sexually parallel cousins—that is, the child of a father's brother or of a mother's sister. Occasionally, one woman might take on more than one husband, usually brothers, and men sometimes made wives of several sisters. These multiple marriages were often intended to sustain those who could not survive on their own.

Dependency was looked down on by most subarctic groups, who, especially in lean times, were dragged down by the helpless members of their bands. It was tolerated by most people only in their children, who were cherished and closely reared by parents and the other adults in the

A necklace made of beads and dentaliums (right) and a caribou-skin hair ornament (below) were indications that a Tahltan girl had reached maturity. She would wear these items until the time of her marriage.

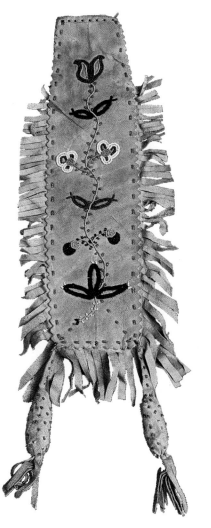

band. Until puberty at least, children were almost never physically disciplined, an easygoing style of parenting that offended Father Le Jeune; he could not imagine a mission school in which children were not now and then punished into obedience and understanding.

Age brought a kind of reverence among the subarctic peoples, but often a dire practical necessity as well. "It is the custom of this tribe," wrote Le Jeune of the Montagnais, "to kill their fathers and mothers when they are so old that they can walk no longer, thinking that they are doing them a good service; for otherwise they would be compelled to die of hunger, as they have become unable to follow the others." Women were considered old when they could no longer keep up on the migratory treks; men, when their legs would not carry them on the hunt. Other groups, such as the Slavey and the Gwich'in, kept their sick and old with them to the end. Still, the realities of life sometimes made their own priorities. When the aged could no longer keep the pace on the winter trail, they asked their family to kill them, and kept asking until their wish had been granted.

The subarctic Indians used a great variety of methods to dispose of their dead. Some groups were caring and fastidious; others seemed blind to the deceased. The migratory tribes, for example, often simply left the dead in their dwelling and moved on to another hunting camp. Chipewyans sometimes did even less, leaving the corpse on the ground without preparation or protection. But such abandonment of the dead was rare, forced by the weakness of the starving survivors. All death, except that inflicted by sorcery, was considered natural.

Cremation was widely used by some Crees and most of the Athapaskan speakers, but not exclusively. The Naskapi buried the corpse sev-

eral feet deep, resting on its side and slightly bent as though sleeping, or placed in a sitting position. Only enemies were buried standing up, because that meant their spirits would find no repose. Blankets and other belongings, and sometimes the body of a dog, were added. In the forest in winter, the dead were laid out on platforms in the trees until the ground thawed sufficiently to bury them.

A woman accompanied by her dog collects snowshoe hares from her traps set in a thicket. The hunting and snaring of smaller game was often woman's work.

Every group differed in their beliefs about the afterlife. Some, like the Gwich'in, believed they were reincarnated in another family and of the opposite sex. The Dogrib held that humans now and then returned as animals—encountering an animal one could not kill seemed proof that the animal had formerly taken human form. The 17th-century Montagnais said that the souls of people went on a long journey, looking for other souls to use; in a sense, their hunting life resumed. "They hunt for the souls of beavers, porcupines, moose, and other animals," a shaman explained to Father Le Jeune, "using the soul of the snowshoes to walk upon the soul of the snow." To many groups, the Milky Way was the Ghost Road that spirits took to the other world. The Slavey thought that loon and otter spirits helped human spirits pass through the earth to resume their lives elsewhere. Mainly, all believed that the human spirit did not end with this world—that life went on in some altered form.

To varying degrees, death was faced with equanimity, partly no doubt because the spirits went somewhere better, but also because the Indians

Hare skins cut into strips and twisted into cords hang from a line. The woman in the background is sewing the hides together to make a blanket. It takes about 50 skins to complete a blanket for one adult.

A young boy wears a jacket that is made entirely of hare skins. Traditionally, women and children among the eastern subarctic groups wore clothing made from hare pelts.

kept their emotions under strict control. Grief was expressed in highly ritualized ways, some of them taking the extreme form of self-mutilation, to show that the loss of a loved one had forever altered the physical world. Although joy was openly expressed at feasts and dances, deep feelings sometimes remained private. In their dealings with strangers, Indians often gave no sign of their emotional state.

"They make a pretense of never getting angry," wrote Le Jeune, "not because of the beauty of this virtue, for which they have not even a name, but for their own contentment and happiness, I mean, to avoid the bitterness caused by anger." Once, the priest said, the shaman in his group claimed, "As for me, nothing can disturb me; let hunger oppress me, let my nearest relation pass to the other life, let the Iroquois, our enemies, massacre our people, I never get angry." Anger was known to be a corrosive emotion.

As there was a resistance to expressing hostility, there was also a reluctance to enter into armed conflict. People who were forced to live one day at a time had neither the time nor the means for mounting an extended campaign against an enemy. The fighting that did occur was short lived. The majority of the groups that lived along the northern timberline skirmished with Eskimos, for example. The Chandalar Gwich'in tell stories of victories over Eskimos and the Dihai Gwich'in, a neighboring group, but these are usually tales of hand-to-hand combat in which the weaponry is limited to caribou-antler clubs, knives, and thrusting spears. Usually the fights were sparked by raiding parties looking for women, weapons, and supplies, or by some lingering wish for vengeance, or a vendetta between families or kinship groups. In the east, the Montagnais and the Cree ritually tortured their captives.

Another, more dangerous enemy was destined to appear. "For generation after generation," recounted a Tanana Indian of the Alaska plateau, "the Indians have heard that a strange, new people were coming to kill the Indians and take away their hunting grounds. These new people would have yellow hair and pale skin. My father told me this story; his father told him; and his father told him."

The new people would bring iron knives, firearms, alcohol, and metal pots for cooking. They would also bring a host of diseases for which the Indians had no immunity—including the malady of avarice, which Le Jeune had found entirely lacking in the Montagnais. They would even bring new names for the people, and for the land and lakes and rivers. They would also bring science and new gods. Something was coming, and it was, in some ways, worse than Windigo. ◆

By the light of a full moon on a winter's night, Windigo, the icy phantom of Northern Ojibwa and Cree legend, devours human beings that it perceives to be beaver in this painting by Ojibwa artist Norval Morrisseau. Beliefs about the cannibal giant may have arisen from the terrible fear that starvation or madness might drive one to consume human flesh.

ON THE TRAIL OF THE BEAVER

Every fall the Mistassini Cree people in the James Bay area of west-central Quebec leave their permanent settlement to camp on their ancestral hunting grounds in the forest. In groups of two or three families, the Mistassini spend six to nine months of the year living off the land passed down to them from kinspeople. They hunt bear, moose, caribou, lynx, marten, otter, porcupine, mink, snowshoe hare, ducks, and geese, and catch fish too. But their main endeavor is trapping beaver, whose meat sustains them and whose valuable fur they trade for material goods they cannot obtain from the forest.

The Mistassini hunters spend months planning the winter hunt, deciding which lands to use and which to rest, where to hunt bear, and which beaver lodges to trap this season, based on information gained the previous spring. They are so accurate in estimating the beaver population each year that the Quebec government uses the Mistassini figures to determine trapping quotas. But along with their detailed scientific knowledge of the land and animals, the Mistassini rely on spiritual techniques to ensure a successful hunt. Dreams, songs to the animals, weather prediction, respectful behavior, and divination methods all help the hunters find their prey.

A bear's shoulder bone, carefully burned over a fire, displays cracks that suggest good hunting areas by their resemblance to known geographical features.

Mistassini hunters make their way through patches of ice on one of four lakes they must cross during a daylong trip to take a census of beaver lodges.

A Mistassini hunter (above) instructs his son in setting a trap near the entrance to a snow-covered beaver lodge. Any slight disturbance of the sticks protruding through the snow will alert the hunter to the presence of a captured beaver.

Steel traps such as the one at near right, known as a Conibear trap after its inventor, are the type most common-ly used by Mistassini hunters. Attracted by willow branches left as bait, the bea-ver swims into the trap, which snaps shut, breaking the animal's back.

A hunter releases a dead beaver from a trap (far right). He will then wipe the carcass on the snow to remove as much water from it as pos-sible before drag-ging it home.

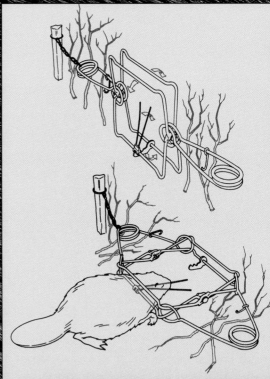

Tying the "nima-pan," or ceremonial string, to the piece of wood threaded through the nose of a beaver, a Mistassini hunter readies his catch for the homeward journey. The wooden plug prevents blood from spilling on the snow, which would show disrespect to the animal's spirit.

This brightly colored nimapan (below), made of four strands of twine braided together with a loop at the end, is the traditional means of dragging beaver and otter back to camp. It is also a symbol of the hunter's spiritual link with the game animals.

With a nimapan looped around his chest, a Mistassini hunter pulls a beaver over the snow. The beaver is placed on its back as a sign of respect.

At the entryway to their lodge (top), a hunter's wife takes her husband's catch, pulling it into the dwelling by the nimapan. Although a beaver is cause for celebration in camp, the children may not run out to greet the returning hunters lest they offend the animal's spirit.

The knife above is used to scrape the skins of beaver and caribou. In the past, such flensing tools were fashioned out of caribou antler, but today they are made of metal.

On a floor of freshly laid spruce boughs covered with a plastic sheet, a Mistassini woman skins a beaver (upper right). The care with which the women prepare the pelts makes Mistassini beaver furs prized around the world.

Beaver skins hanging on stretchers dry in the freezing air as a hunter and his child admire these gifts from the forest. When dried, the pelts will be removed from the stretchers and carefully stored, awaiting the airborne arrival of the fur trader.

GOOD HUNTING WITH HELP FROM THE SPIRITS

To Crees, as to many other Native Americans, there is more to hunting than tracking and killing an animal. The spiritual dimension of the hunt is just as important as the physical; indeed, the Cree believe that only through the spirits can future success in hunting be ensured. By showing respect for his prey, the hunter pleases the spirits who control the game animals. In return, those spirits reward the hunter by sending him more prey.

Showing respect means following a complex set of rules, such as not pointing at an animal or walking in its footprints when tracking it. It means bringing home the animal quietly, without celebration, and displaying the carcass in the lodge. It also means honoring the animal with a feast, placing food offerings in the fire, and giving the bones back to the spirits by hanging them in a tree.

Some of these rules have originated in tribal legends. In the Cree legend of The Boy Who Was Kept by a Bear, a father sets out to kill the bear that has captured his son. The bear attempts to distract the hunter by throwing various other game animals out of the den. But the father ignores the animals and continues on his quest for the bear. "I cannot defeat him!" cries the bear. "Straight! Straight! He comes walking to me." Realizing he is about to be killed, the bear gives the boy a gift of one of his forelegs, telling him that if he wraps it carefully and keeps it hanging in a certain place, he will always be able to find bear. The boy follows these instructions and becomes such a successful bear hunter that he is able to feed his hunting group entirely on bear meat.

From this story evolved the Cree taboo against going after other animals when engaged in a bear hunt, and the tale explains why the bear's forelegs are given special treatment. Even today, the forelegs are cooked separately, and the bones are carefully wrapped and hung in a tree. Thus are the spirits appeased.

A hunter sits near the head of a young caribou that he has recently killed (below). When an animal is brought into a dwelling to be displayed, it is placed at the rear of the lodge with its head facing the door, in what is considered the seat of honor.

The bear below is displayed on a bed of freshly cut spruce boughs atop a tarpaulin. The internal organs have been removed to keep the meat from spoiling. At feasts to honor the bear, the animal's grease is served, using a ceremonial ladle such as the one at left.

After feasting, a Cree hunter takes his turn
at the drum, offering songs of thanksgiving
for a successful hunt. The drum frequently
hangs from the ceiling on a cord, by which
its songs may ascend to the spirits.

After killing a bear,
hunters gather
around the animal
and smoke tobacco,
often with a ceremo-
nial pipe such as the
one at right. They
place an offering of
tobacco on the
bear's chest, thank-
ing the prey for its
gift to them.

Beaver skulls are fastened on the trunk of a tree growing beside a lake in Quebec. The view of a lake is said to please the spirits of water-dwelling animals. Skulls are placed high to keep other animals from desecrating them.

A set of caribou antlers decorated with ribbons (above) sits on a special platform in a tree near a hunting camp. Skulls of small mammals hang from the platform. The antlers are oriented to face the rising sun.

A bear skull (left), thought to hold the concentrated power of a bear after death, is often painted or marked with burned wood before being hung in a tree. Passing hunters leave tobacco in the skull's nostrils. The skin from a bear's chin (below) is made into a pouch containing a bit of bear flesh and carried as a powerful hunting charm.

The leader of a Cree hunting party (left) checks the birch-bark-wrapped package of bear forelegs he has just fastened to a tree. Bear forelegs might also be hung above a hunter's sleeping place in the lodge to induce good dreams.

The bones of small mammals, such as hare, hang from a small tree near a hunting camp (right), giving notice to the spirits that the people in this place honor the animals.

The stuffed and decorated head of a Canada goose was carried as an amulet to promote good hunting. Such an amulet was usually made by a young hunter's mother after he presented her with his first goose.

A specially constructed platform (left) keeps the bones of land animals killed by hunters out of reach of scavenging dogs. Such platforms are left as permanent displays of respect after the hunting group moves on.

2

A SHATTERING OF AGE-OLD TRADITIONS

Laden with furs, Hudson's Bay Company freight boats ply rough waters en route to Hudson Bay, where the goods will be transferred to larger vessels. The sail of one boat is decorated with an Indian design. The company issued tokens for trading and gambling. The holes indicate that this one (above, left), shown front and back, may have been used as an ornament.

In July 1534, a band of Indians summering on what would soon be known as the Gaspé Peninsula, a broad tongue of Canada that juts into the Gulf of Saint Lawrence, spied two sailing ships anchored in a small cove off the south coast. The Indians were Micmacs, Algonquian-speaking people who hunted and fished the rivers of the Maritime Provinces, following the rhythms of the seasons like their neighbors to the north, the Montagnais of Labrador, and the Beothuk of the Island of Newfoundland.

Now and again over the past three decades, all three groups had encountered pale-skinned strangers—Breton, Norman, and Basque cod fishermen from across the sea. Some of these foreigners were in the habit of coming ashore from their high-masted vessels to salt their catch on the beach. The Indians had begun a lucrative trade with them, exchanging their animal skins for items of great beauty and usefulness.

Word of the tall ships must have caused a flurry of excitement in the Micmac camp, for it offered a rare opportunity to acquire iron tools that were more durable and efficient than their own implements of stone, bone, wood, bark, and antler. The Micmacs placed their furs on sticks, held them aloft, and gestured to the seafarers to come ashore. But these white men were in no mood to barter. They responded to the friendly overtures by firing two small cannonballs over the Micmacs' heads. The thunderlike claps sent the Indians scattering.

The Micmacs were undeterred. The following day, they returned and again signaled their desire to trade. This time the foreigners understood. By nightfall the Indians had bartered away all of their skins, including even the ones they were wearing, in exchange for some iron hatchets and knives, glass beads, and a red cap for the man the French perceived to be their leader. Some of the women rubbed the arms of the seamen as if they hoped to acquire some of the strangers' medicine. Other Micmacs showed their pleasure by throwing salt water over their heads, dancing, and performing other ceremonies that the Frenchmen did not understand. The trading session had gone well, and to the Indians, it must have seemed much the same as their previous encounters with whites. Yet this meeting was fundamentally different from all the others.

These foreigners were not fishermen, but French explorers under the command of a 43-year-old pilot named Jacques Cartier who had embarked on a voyage of discovery for their king. They were looking for a water passage through the "Terre Neuve" to Asia, a route that would lead them to "certain isles and countries" where it was said there were "great quantities of gold and riches." Cartier and his men had already worked their way along the coast of what is today eastern Quebec, taking soundings and probing inlets and rivers, in an effort to piece together a cartographic picture of the New Land. Instead of a route to Asia, however, they had found only dead ends. The Frenchmen had little interest in the animal skins offered them in trade. All they wanted was information about waterways leading west. But this was impossible to communicate, given each party's ignorance of the other's language. The two groups went their separate ways: the Micmacs continuing the age-old business of survival, the Frenchmen on their ambitious quest.

Before Cartier sailed for home later on that summer, he would explore the northern shore of the gulf and encounter representatives of two other indigenous groups: a community of Saint Lawrence Valley Iroquois, who had come up from their village of Stadacona to lay in a supply of fish for the winter; and a band of nomadic hunters, probably Montagnais. The

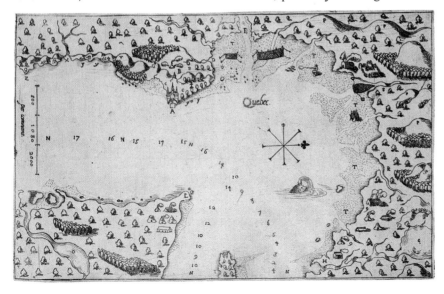

A map drawn by Samuel de Champlain shows the area around the French settlement at Quebec (marked "A") as it appeared in the years 1608-1612. The French explorer included details of Montagnais life, such as their conical and domed lodges, an eel net at the mouth of a river, and two fishnets on nearby tidal flats.

Montagnais had obviously dealt with white men before. They behaved so familiarly, Cartier subsequently wrote, that they came "as freely aboard our vessels as if they had been Frenchmen."

No one knows what the 16th-century Indians of the Saint Lawrence gulf region thought of the Europeans they encountered. The only existing lore comes from the Micmac in the form of a dream by a young woman from a Prince Edward Island band. Parts of the dream describe the arrival of a masted ship as a small island of tall trees drifting in toward shore. It seemed that bears were climbing in the branches of the trees. When the men in her band reached for their weapons, the bears became human beings, some of whom lowered a strange-looking canoe into the water and paddled ashore.

To Cartier the Indians were an uncultivated folk. He deemed their clothing and hunting gear rudimentary, and dismissed their furs as articles of "little value." Of the Indians he saw along the Labrador coast, he wrote: "These men may very well and truely be called Wilde, because there is no poorer people in the world. For I thinke all that they had together, besides their boats and nets, was not worth five souce. They go altogether naked saving their privities, which are covered with a little skinne, and certaine olde skinnes that they cast upon them." He smugly predicted that these primitives "would be easy to convert to our holy faith."

The following year, Cartier returned to the gulf and, guided by the Iroquois, found exactly what he had been seeking—an enormous waterway that led westward to a land the Indians called Canada. He dubbed it Rivière de Canada, a name that would later be changed to the Saint Lawrence. Cartier traveled up the river as far as the Iroquois village of Hochelaga, near the site of the modern city of Montreal. A new era was dawning. The great river would indeed lead to riches, but not in gold and gemstones, as the explorers had envisioned. The wealth would be in furs—the very commodity Cartier had scorned.

In 1541 Cartier made a third voyage to Canada, this time to establish a permanent French colony on behalf of King Francis I, who needed an outpost to help him compete for New World holdings with his Spanish and Portuguese rivals. To secure the blessing of the Vatican, the French professed religious motives for the expedition. Their objective, they claimed, was neither land nor money nor power, but the desire to propagate Chris-

A Montagnais girl wears an old-style, handsewn hat known as a tuque. It is made of six pieces of alternately colored cloth and sits atop the head with the upper portion folded over on itself.

tianity and, as King Francis I put it, to save "an infinity of souls for God."

For the king's settlement, Cartier chose a point overlooking the Saint Lawrence River, near the location of the modern city of Quebec (an Indian name meaning "narrows"). He named the colony Charlesbourg Royal and the point Cap aux Diamants (Cape Diamond) because he expected to mine precious stones from its heights. Although the Iroquois living in the nearby village of Stadacona had befriended Cartier six years earlier, they felt threatened by him now and began to harass the settlers. After a harsh winter, in the face of growing Iroquois hostility, Cartier abandoned the supposedly permanent colony and sailed for France. On his return, he crossed paths with the colony's new governor, a nobleman with the title of Sieur de Roberval, who had been delayed. Although dismayed by Cartier's retreat, Roberval and his party pressed on; they endured one winter in Canada before giving up and returning to France in 1543.

Over the course of the next several decades, however, French fishermen continued to ply Canadian waters for cod and trade for furs with the Indians. As more and more of these pelts passed from hand to hand in Europe, they no longer were looked upon as exotic curiosities. Clothing manufacturers began experimenting with them, and when French hat makers discovered that beaver skins could be converted into stylish hats, the pelts became valuable. What the hatters prized was not the visible fur, the long and coarse hair of the outer coat, but rather the soft velvety undercoat that lay next to the animal's skin.

The Indians normally harvested beaver in winter when their pelts were at their most luxuriant. The women processed the hides by scraping them and rubbing them with animal marrow. They cut the hides into rectangles and sewed five to eight of them together to make leggings or coats. The garments were worn with the fur next to the body for maximum warmth. After about a year and a half of wear, the outer hair wore off, exposing the undercoat. These skins, later called *castor gras d'hiver,* or "coat beaver," were the ones that the hatters coveted. The ordinary, air-dried pelts, later known as *castor sec,* or "parchment beaver," were valued less because they took longer to process into felt for hats.

During the summer of 1583, a French merchant by the name of Étienne Bellenger sailed to Cape Breton on Nova Scotia and in short order assembled a cargo of furs that sold for 10 times the value of the goods he traded for them. Entranced by Bellenger's profits, a consortium of merchants sent five ships up the Saint Lawrence the next summer. When they came back laden with furs that sold at a similar profit, the merchants or-

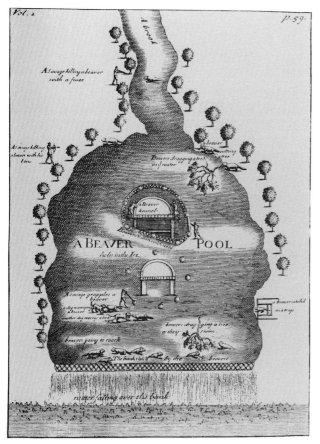

This 1703 engraving illustrates various methods of hunting beaver. The easiest time to catch beaver was winter, when ice limited the animals' movements. After blocking the entryways, the Indians broke into the lodge and killed the escaping animals, sometimes spearing them through holes cut in the ice. In open water, they snared beaver in nets placed over the lodge entrances.

ganized a fleet of 10 vessels for the following year. The traders were in a frenzy, not only to find new sources of pelts but also to obtain royal approval for their enterprise. An industry had been born.

The rise of the fur trade would have profound consequences for the subarctic peoples. The French and later the English would establish networks of trading posts that would eventually stretch across Canada. Group by group and band by band, beginning with the eastern Algonquians and eventually including many of the western Athapaskans, the Indians would find their age-old traditions threatened by foreigners whose notions of personal property, wealth, family ties, and religion were utterly alien from their own. Yet, disparate though the Indians and the Europeans were in their lifestyles and outlook, the production of furs would provide a common ground that would allow them to coexist and work together. Intermarriages between Indian women and white men would begin early and play a major role in advancing the fur trade across Canada by creating close bonds between the traders and the women's kin.

The Indians would provide the Europeans not only with furs but also with food and natural know-how that would enable the newcomers to survive. In addition, they would serve the traders as guides, couriers, laborers, and transporters of goods. In return, the Indians would receive manufactured goods that would alleviate their toil but irrevocably alter their lives.

In 1603 a French expedition that included a 36-year-old navigator by the name of Samuel de Champlain returned to the Saint Lawrence Valley to make another attempt at colonization. The French quickly discovered that great changes had taken place among the native population. There were no longer any permanent villages along the great river. The Laurentian Iroquois had mysteriously disappeared, supplanted by an alliance of Algonquian-speaking hunting peoples, including the Micmac, the Algonquin of the Ottawa River region, the Etchemin, or Penobscot, of the southern shore of the Saint Lawrence, and the Montagnais.

The Montagnais flourished as full partners in the French fur trade, especially at the trading center of Tadoussac at the mouth of the Saguenay River, which joins the Saint Lawrence about 100 miles downstream from the site of Cartier and Roberval's aborted settlement of Charlesbourg

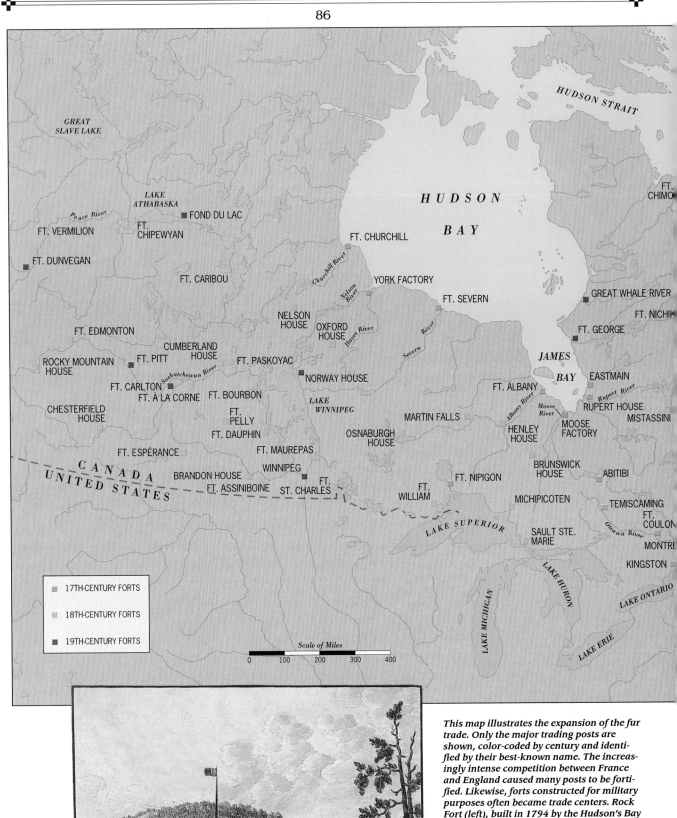

GREAT
SLAVE LAKE

FT. VERMILION

FT. DUNVEGAN

Peace River

LAKE
ATHABASKA

FT.
CHIPEWYAN

■ FOND DU LAC

HUDSON STRAIT

HUDSON

BAY

FT. CHURCHILL

FT.
CHIMO

Churchill River

FT. CARIBOU

Nelson River

YORK FACTORY

GREAT WHALE RIVER

FT. SEVERN

FT. NICHIK

FT. EDMONTON

NELSON
HOUSE

OXFORD
HOUSE

Hayes River

Severn River

FT. GEORGE

ROCKY MOUNTAIN
HOUSE

CUMBERLAND
HOUSE

FT. PITT

FT. PASKOYAC

Saskatchewan River

NORWAY HOUSE

JAMES

BAY

EASTMAIN

FT. ALBANY

Albany River

*Moose
River*

RUPERT HOUSE

Rupert River

MISTASSINI

FT. CARLTON
FT. À LA CORNE

FT. BOURBON

CHESTERFIELD
HOUSE

FT.
PELLY

LAKE
WINNIPEG

MARTIN FALLS

HENLEY
HOUSE

MOOSE
FACTORY

FT. DAUPHIN

OSNABURGH
HOUSE

FT. ESPÉRANCE

FT. MAUREPAS

BRUNSWICK
HOUSE

ABITIBI

WINNIPEG

C A N A D A

BRANDON HOUSE

FT. NIPIGON

UNITED STATES

FT. ASSINIBOINE

FT.
ST. CHARLES

FT.
WILLIAM

MICHIPICOTEN

TEMISCAMING
FT.
COULON

Ottawa River

MONTRE

LAKE SUPERIOR

SAULT STE.
MARIE

KINGSTON

■ 17TH-CENTURY FORTS

■ 18TH-CENTURY FORTS

■ 19TH-CENTURY FORTS

Scale of Miles

0   100   200   300   400

LAKE MICHIGAN

LAKE HURON

LAKE ONTARIO

LAKE ERIE

This map illustrates the expansion of the fur trade. Only the major trading posts are shown, color-coded by century and identified by their best-known name. The increasingly intense competition between France and England caused many posts to be fortified. Likewise, forts constructed for military purposes often became trade centers. Rock Fort (left), built in 1794 by the Hudson's Bay Company on the Hayes River about 120 miles southwest of York Factory on Hudson Bay, was a depot for smaller inland posts.

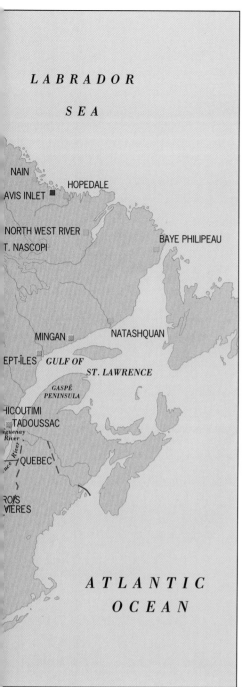

LABRADOR

SEA

NAIN

HOPEDALE

AVIS INLET

NORTH WEST RIVER

T. NASCOPI

BAYE PHILIPEAU

MINGAN   NATASHQUAN

EPT-ÎLES   GULF OF

ST. LAWRENCE

GASPÉ
PENINSULA

HICOUTIMI

TADOUSSAC

Saguenay
River

QUEBEC

ROIS
VIERES

ATLANTIC

OCEAN

Royal. The Saguenay tapped a rich hinterland. In addition to harvesting their own beaver resources, the Montagnais soon became effective middlemen, acquiring pelts from bands in the interior and then trading them to the French. The Montagnais also learned to exploit the competition for pelts between rival traders. They refused to barter any of their winter's stock until all of the expected French ships had arrived at Tadoussac for the summer's trading, thus creating a bidding war that drove prices so high that some of the white traders could not afford to participate. Decades later, Jesuit priest Paul Le Jeune reported a Montagnais jokingly telling him, "The beaver does everything perfectly well; it makes kettles, hatchets, swords, knives, bread; and in short, it makes everything." Another mocked the English, who had by that time joined the competition for furs. "The English have no sense," he told Le Jeune. "They gave us 20 knives like this for one beaver skin."

Exploring the lower reaches of the Saguenay River in 1603, Champlain learned about the network of lakes and rivers to the northwest along which the Montagnais gathered pelts for trade—from Indian bands so far away, it was said, that they were "within sight of a saltwater sea." Champlain discounted the notion that his informants were describing the long-sought route to Asia. Instead, he declared flatly that they meant another bay or gulf on the Atlantic "whose waters enter from the North into the lands and in truth it can be nothing else."

Later on, pushing up the Saint Lawrence to the site of the former Iroquois village of Hochelaga, Champlain (who, unlike Cartier in 1535, had the benefit of interpreters) heard descriptions of other trade routes, up the Ottawa River to the land of the Algonquin and the Huron, and along a series of great lakes (Ontario and Erie), leading to a strait that linked to an enormous, salty lake whose farthest extent was unknown to the local Montagnais. This, Champlain thought, might be the long-sought *mer du Su,* or Asia Sea, leading to the Orient. It was, in fact, today's Lake Huron.

Champlain set up his headquarters at Quebec in 1608. His objective, in addition to pushing westward to find that tantalizing mer du Su, was to get control of the trade routes leading to the interior. These were jealously guarded by the Montagnais, who set up every obstacle they could think of to prevent the French from traveling inland and refused to allow faraway Indian bands to reach the French without dealing first with them. Although the Indians normally permitted other bands to use their hunting grounds when they were not exploiting them, rights of passage for trade always had to be negotiated. The Montagnais enforced this rule with in-

A WAY OF WALKING ON SNOW

Perhaps no piece of technology was more important to the subarctic Indians than the snowshoe. This marvelous invention, attributed in a Chipewyan creation story to the first man and first woman, allowed the Indians to move freely and easily over deep, soft snow by distributing the weight of the body over a broader surface.

Although the simplest versions were made of a wooden slab and a hide thong, most snowshoes consisted of a birch frame, shaved and bent into shape by the men, with an intricate netting made from strips of partially tanned caribou or moose hide, laced by the women through predrilled holes. Customarily, the men did the lacing of the central section that bore the weight of the foot, using a thicker gauge of hide.

Snowshoes came in a variety of shapes and sizes that were almost as great as the number of different groups that used them. Generally, the Indians favored long, narrow snowshoes with the toes either flat or curled and the ends either pointed or rounded. When wearing these styles in open terrain, the snowshoer walks with long, swinging strides, lifting the toes and letting the tail or heel of the snowshoe drag. The upturned styles are particularly good for breaking trail. In the East, the Montagnais and Naskapi traditionally preferred oval-shaped snowshoes with very short tails or no tail at all, styles that allowed them to maneuver in hilly, densely wooded and brush-filled terrain.

An Athapaskan child walks on his own pint-size snowshoes in 1912. The size of the snowshoe depends on the weight of the wearer.

The bone tools in this leather holder were used by a Southern Tutchone woman to work snowshoe lacing. They include two awls, one of which is wrapped in strips of hide; a netting needle; and a hooking tool.

A Montagnais woman of the Pointe Bleue band laces a swallowtail snowshoe, a style used on trails and in early winter and spring. Many Indians carry more than one type of snowshoe with them for different snow conditions.

Cree boys learn how to make snowshoes at their school in Mistassini, Quebec. The designs in the weave are pleasing to the spirits, enabling the snowshoes to better carry their wearer. The wool tassels on the frame serve a similar purpose, in addition to muffling the sound of crunching through the snow's crust.

A Slavey man demonstrates how to put on a pair of snowshoes. He inserts his foot into the harness (left), then adjusts the fit by tightening the single-loop bowknot that lies outside the forefoot (below). He is wearing flexible moccasins—the best footwear for walking on snowshoes.

Subarctic snowshoes vary by frame shape and weave. Each style was suited to a particular terrain and type of snow. The samples shown here include (clockwise from top right): swallowtail, elbow, wooden, pointed toe, round toe, bearpaw, and beaver tail.

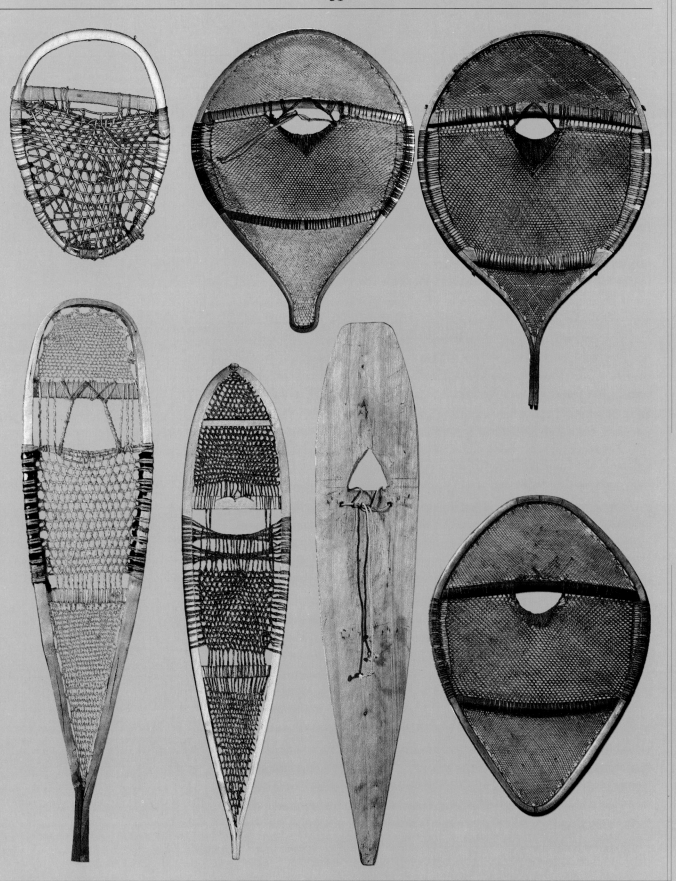

creasing vigor as they depleted the beaver in their own territory. Thus did the Montagnais experience set a pattern that would be followed again and again as Europeans pressed westward.

Already the Indians and Europeans involved in the fur trade had profoundly affected one another. For their part, the French had come to appreciate the continent for the wealth it had to offer, and they had gained greater respect for its inhabitants. Schooled by the Indians, the French fur traders were learning how to travel freely in the vast boreal forest, using birch-bark canoes on rivers and lakes in summer, snowshoes and toboggans on the deep snows of winter. They got used to eating moose, caribou, and beaver. They tried smoking tobacco and, before long, as a disgusted Jesuit reported, became "so bewitched with it that to drink of this smoke they would sell their shirts from their backs." Another observer noted that once Frenchmen were accustomed to tobacco, "they can no more be without it than without meat or drink."

Such changes were minor, however, compared with the transformation of Montagnais life that occurred within a few decades of contact with the French. The first casualty was the austere regimen, developed over millennia, with which the Montagnais had adapted to their subarctic environment. Traditionally, Montagnais families had traveled familiar routes within relatively small areas, following an annual routine of hunting and gathering. They had moved across the land as if guests at a great buffet, sampling fish in the summer, eel and bear in the fall, porcupine and beaver in early winter, caribou and moose in late winter, geese and partridge in the spring, eating their fill, and moving on. Because they did not rely heavily on any particular area or species for their food supply, they never risked obliterating any single kind of animal, nor were they threatened when some animal went into a decline, as, for example, the snowshoe hare periodically did.

When they started trading with the French, life changed. Hours of honing edges on stone knives, scrapers, hatchets, and arrow points were obviated by the availability of metal knives, hatchets, arrowheads, and especially guns. The owner of a flint-and-steel could make fire anywhere without having to transport embers; a woman who had an iron kettle no longer had to make bark vessels and heat their contents with hot rocks; it was much easier to decorate clothing and accessories with ready-made glass beads than to gather, polish, and mount seashells and porcupine quills.

The Montagnais used the time and energy saved from processing food and fiber to adapt to the new facts of their life. They began a relent-

A man, probably a Cree, from the Great Whale River region of northern Quebec, smokes a Montagnais-style pipe similar to that painted by William Hind, an artist on the Canadian government expedition to Labrador in 1861 (inset). A decorative beaded cord links the carved stone bowl to the stem.

less pursuit of the beaver. Although they still drew on the whole range of animal life in their environment, taking from each species a little of what they needed for survival, the focus of life became their relations with French traders. The labor-saving innovations were thought of by Europeans as improvements in the Montagnais standard of living. But once the exacting skills of subsistence were lost, they could not be easily revived when trade was interrupted by, for example, the failure of a supply ship to make the Atlantic crossing on time. In such an event, the previously self-sufficient people sometimes suffered from famine.

The new emphasis on killing beaver as an item of trade to exchange for all the needs of the band altered the Indians' traditional relationships with the earth and its creatures. Gradually, the supply of prime beaver in their home grounds declined. In order to satisfy the demand for more pelts, the Montagnais were forced to range farther afield, bringing them into greater contact with other bands.

Worse still, prolonged contact with the French explorers and traders introduced the Indians to a variety of infectious diseases—influenza, smallpox, measles—against which they had no defenses. "They are astonished and often complain," reported the Jesuit priest Pierre Biard in 1616, "that since the French mingle with them and carry on trade with them they are dying fast and the population is thinning out."

While the French may not have intended to restructure the Montagnais' material life, they deliberately set out to reorient their spiritual life. As the fur trade developed, the increasing number of traders was paralleled by an influx of missionaries, most of them Jesuits, who found it was much more difficult to change beliefs than work habits. Father Paul Le Jeune, who for about a quarter-century beginning in 1632 was the father superior of all Jesuit missionaries in New France, lamented the difficulty of appealing to a people who seemed to need nothing: They were "harmonious among themselves," he wrote, "rendering no homage to any one whomsoever, except when they like." Moreover, "as they are contented with a mere living, not one of them gives himself to the Devil to acquire wealth."

There were other Montagnais traits that made deep, positive impressions on the Jesuits, belying Cartier's negative view of the Indians 100 years earlier. "In Paris we cannot sleep without the doors well bolted," Father Biard wrote after he returned to France from Canada. "But there we close them against the wind only, and sleep no less securely." Commenting on the Montagnais character, another priest wrote: "They have courage, fidelity, generosity, and humanity, and their hospitality is so innate and praiseworthy that they receive among them every man who is not an enemy. These are not simpletons like many people over here; they speak with much judgment and good sense; so that if we commonly call them savages, the word is abusive and unmerited."

One of the greatest frustrations of the missionaries was that the Indians recognized no hierarchies. No one seemed to be in charge, either in the household or in the band; no one enunciated or enforced rules of behavior, even among the children. Rather, everyone was given the opportunity to participate fully in the life and the decisions of the community.

This print of a watercolor by a Métis artist in 1805 depicts a snowshoeing couple with a dog pulling their toboggan. The woman, probably a Cree, carries a cradleboard on her back. The man, possibly a white trader, carries a gun and ax.

The Jesuits were implacable in urging the Montagnais to give and obey orders—husbands to wives, parents to children, leaders to followers—and to forsake their rich and complex spirit world in favor of the Christian God. The Indians had little understanding of Catholicism, although many of them seemed interested in its trappings—the candles, bells, holy water, and funeral processions. Some Montagnais, according to one priest, treated the sacrament of baptism as if it were "sort of a sacred pledge of friendship and alliance with the French"—a logical conclusion given the Indian tradition of trading only with friends. Others listened politely to the Jesuits' preaching, but then insisted on reciprocity. "They said that when I prayed to God they greatly approved of it, as well as of what I told them," recalled Father Le Jeune, "and hence, that I must also approve of their customs, and I must believe in their ways of doing things." The shamans, in particular, clung tenaciously to the traditions of their ancestors. But the Montagnais customs were crumbling under the onslaught of

A man & his Wife returning with a load of Partridges from their Tents.— By Wm Richards

trade goods, liquor, disease, and dramatically changed ways of doing things. Before long, one Montagnais convert to Christianity proclaimed, "We have burned all our songs, all our dances, all our superstitions and everything that the Devil has taught our forefathers."

After the fur trade had transformed their lives, it passed them by. As the Montagnais had replaced the Micmac as the primary business partners of the French, so they were replaced by the Huron, whom the French had found in the Ottawa River country. Now the Montagnais, with most of their beaver gone and almost all of their trade with other Indians wrested from them, found themselves largely reduced to a humiliating dependence on the charity of French traders and missionaries.

South of the Saint Lawrence, the Iroquois were acting as agents for Dutch fur traders who were working out of the Hudson River valley. By the 1640s, they had exhausted their supply of beaver and, in the pattern now becoming familiar, were forced to become middlemen in the trade. But in the Indian cultures, there was no such thing as trade between people who were not allies, and so the Iroquois took what they wanted by force from their age-old enemies, the Huron and the Algonquin. Over a period of 10 years, they dispersed both groups and terrorized the southern Saint Lawrence River valley on their annual forays for furs.

The French who adapted best to wilderness life, who learned the Indian ways of travel and self-sufficiency, became known as *coureurs de bois*, or "runners of the woods." As the fur trade gained momentum, they ranged ever farther inland in search of new sources of better furs. In the middle of the 17th century, among the best of the coureurs de bois were Sieur de Groseilliers and Pierre Radisson. During a series of westward expeditions that took them as far as Lake Superior in the winter of 1659-1660, Radisson and Groseilliers tried to contact and establish trade with the Indians who had formerly dealt with the Huron but had retreated northward and westward in the face of Iroquois aggression. The Frenchmen learned in their travels of a people who lived northwest of Montagnais territory, along the rivers flowing into Hudson Bay and its lower appendage, James Bay. In their forested northern uplands, beaver were plentiful and of prime quality.

These people would become known to history as the Cree. The Cree who lived to the east of James Bay were in fact more closely related to the Montagnais, but were grouped by 19th-century scholars with the Cree who lived on the western shore of Hudson Bay. Later government and church policies reinforced the mistaken classification.

Radisson and Groseilliers conceived of a far better way of doing business with the James Bay people. The adventurers proposed that French traders, instead of making the tortuous trip by canoe up and down the higher reaches of the Saint Lawrence and its tributaries, take their trade goods by ship through the Hudson Strait into Hudson Bay, thence into James Bay to make an exchange at the mouths of the rivers that drained the surrounding country. The two coureurs de bois took their idea to Quebec, and then to France, but after five years of trying, they had won no support from their compatriots. When they turned in frustration to the English (whose explorers had discovered and named both Hudson and James Bays earlier in the century), they immediately were given financing for a trading voyage. Although one of the vessels was forced to turn back, the other, the ketch *Nonsuch* with Groseilliers aboard, sailed into James Bay in 1668, spent the winter there at the mouth of the river the Frenchmen named the Rupert, and returned in the fall of 1669 with a full cargo of furs.

Immediately, the consortium of investors financing the company requested and were granted a royal monopoly on trade in the area defined in their charter as "all the lands, countries, and territories upon the coasts and confines of the seas" opening on the Hudson Strait. Without regard for

Indians, possibly Saulteaux, welcome an Anglican missionary to their encampment near Lake Winnipeg in 1821. Until the 19th century, so few missionaries ventured into fur-trading territory that Hudson's Bay Company employees jokingly claimed the initials H.B.C. stood for "Here before Christ."

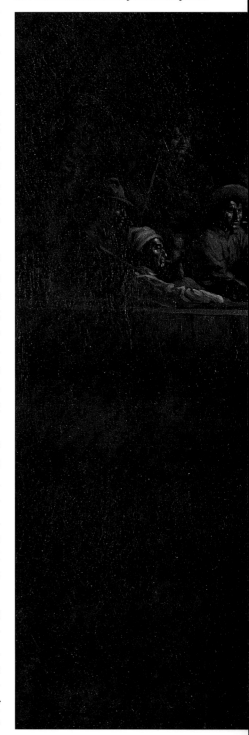

French voyageurs transporting trade goods in a large freight canoe take a break from paddling to enjoy a smoke. In the early 1600s, Samuel de Champlain recognized the superiority of the Indians' lightweight birch-bark canoes over the cumbersome French boats, especially in running rapids and portaging, and advocated their use by his countrymen.

any native population, or residents from other countries, the British charter of 1670 conferred upon the "governor and company of adventurers of England" not only exclusive rights to the region's trade, but the status of "absolute lords and proprietors" over three million square miles of territory.

Two years later, the British returned to Hudson Bay with three ships, laden this time not only with trade goods but also with building supplies, with which they erected a trading post and a warehouse. Although at first they did not stay during the winter months, within 10 years the Hudson's Bay Company had built and occupied three permanent trading posts along the southern shore of James Bay—at the mouths of the Rupert, Moose, and Albany Rivers. From these stockaded forts, or "factories," as they were called, the company was soon shipping more than 10,000 beaver pelts to England each year.

The French, of course, were not pleased to learn that the English were beginning to divert valuable trade to Hudson Bay. Repeatedly during the 1670s, coureurs de bois made their way overland from the Saint Lawrence to James Bay, a trip that required some 200 portages, in order to intercept Crees on their way to the English trading posts. Even though the two European countries were officially at peace, their traders became increasingly hostile. In order to ward off the French threat, the company kept its ships hovering near its forts, with guns trained on the approaches, and established two additional factories on the western shore of the Hudson Bay, at the mouths of the Severn and Nelson Rivers.

The French had trouble maintaining their challenge, however. For one thing, the government of New France became intent on securing outposts and developing the fur trade along the Mississippi River far to the south. And for another, the market, which for nearly a century had been insatiable, fell out of balance. Inventories of the less valuable pelts called parchment beaver became temporarily glutted. By the 1670s, when the market in France was demanding 40,000 of the finer coat beaver and 20,000 parchment beaver each year, French traders were getting 90,000 parchment and only 4,000 coat.

When the French learned that the Hudson's Bay Company was getting mostly coat beaver from the previously untapped markets to the northwest, and that the pelts were of superior quality due to the colder winters, competition resumed with a vengeance. In the 1680s, actual hostilities commenced with armed struggles between the French and the English for possession of the trading posts. In 1686 a French force took possession of all three British forts on James Bay, leaving the Hudson's Bay Company

only its two factories farther north on the western shore of Hudson Bay.

The English traders were at a great disadvantage. Unlike the French, they had not had the time to adapt to the country or its residents, and were not inclined to follow the French example in learning Indian woodcraft and exploring the back country. When a young Englishman named Henry Kelsey traveled westward into the interior in 1690, bringing back accounts of distant groups of Indians with more beaver, the officials of the Hudson's Bay Company ignored him.

As a consequence, English goods spread inland at a slower pace than had been the case with French trading along the Saint Lawrence, and the effect on the Indians was not so precipitate. The English remained dependent for their livelihood on friendly Indians and the annual supply ship from home. They were neither prepared nor motivated to resist French attacks. York Factory, established in 1684 where the Hayes and Nelson Rivers entered Hudson Bay, changed hands six times by 1697.

The James Bay people often were able to take advantage of the competition between the European rivals. The Cree had been trading with the Montagnais for many years and knew the value of the various furs. Although the English treated the Cree fairly and offered a reliable supply of high-quality goods, when the French began to appear in Cree country offering better prices on cloth and gunpowder, the Cree used the offers to make greater demands on the English. They then did business with whichever side gave them the best prices.

Other effects of the European rivalry were far from benign. The French, and then the English, began to use brandy as an inducement to close sales. Like other Native Americans, the subarctic Indians were unprepared for the ravages of alcohol, and wherever it came into play, drunkenness, especially in the form of wild binge drinking, became rampant. Sometimes, after the Indians had become dependent on firearms, the supply of ammunition was cut off, with devastating effect. In 1695, for example, the Hudson's Bay Company did not send out a ship because of a temporary glut of furs. In 1713, while the French held York Factory, they suffered a similar interruption. A visitor reported that they spent the winter "not daring to go outside. They had no goods and their trade was at a standstill, with their Indians dying around them for lack of powder and shot."

But such devastating interruptions were the exception, as the English did their best to impose order on the trade. Most important, they established the beaver pelt as an official currency. A beaver's fur was, of course, fuller during winter than it was in summer, and in the trade the "made

Carrying his catch, a Cree hunter and his family return to York Factory, a major trading post situated on the western shore of Hudson Bay. Their clothing and accouterments reflect a blending of European and Indian influences.

beaver"—the coat of a prime beaver, taken in winter—became the standard by which the values of trade goods and of other furs were defined. The Hudson's Bay Company published an official standard of trade, a catalog that listed the price in made beaver of every item of trade goods and of every kind of pelt. One made beaver, for example, could buy five pounds of shot or tobacco, a dozen needles, eight knives, or two hatchets. It took six made beaver to buy a blanket and 12 to purchase a four-foot-long firearm. Smaller weapons could be purchased with 10 or 11 made beaver.

The standard of trade was official only between the trading posts and the company; the traders kept for themselves any advantage they could gain over the Indians by demanding more furs for specific articles. This profit was called the overplus. These side commissions were eagerly sought but hard to come by, because the Indians were well versed in the going prices and never hesitated to play off one trader against another.

At the Hudson's Bay Company posts, the trading season could not begin until the rivers shook loose their burden of ice, which usually occurred early in March. Then the season began slowly, with the first to arrive at the posts with their winter's take of furs being those who lived closest to the bay, where beaver were less plentiful. Later, larger parties with larger quantities of furs arrived from farther inland.

The English, like the French, were uncomfortable dealing with large numbers of individual Indians and, as a result, insisted on appointing an Indian leader to negotiate for the owners of the pelts. The Europeans selected men who looked to them to be persons of authority, dressed them in European finery, addressed them as "captain," and then demanded to deal only with them. As long as the prices were right, the Indians were content to go along with this routine, but as one British trader noted, they afforded their so-called captains only "trifling respect," which they dropped as soon as they were out of sight of the trading post or camp.

The lack of authority in Cree culture continued to mystify the Europeans, especially the class-conscious English. They often wondered how the Indians ever got anything done. "They have no manner of government or subordination amongst them," one late-18th-century English trader mused. "The father or head of a family owns no superior, obeys no command. When several tents or families meet to go to war, or to the factories to trade, they choose a leader; but it is only a voluntary obedience. They follow him with fidelity and execute his projects with alacrity; but their obedience does not follow from any right in the leader to command but what is founded on his merit, the affections of his followers, and the desire of subduing their antagonists."

The Cree also managed to force the Europeans to honor Indian trading customs. Before any exchanges began, an arriving group of Indians required the traders to participate in a ritual exchange of speeches, pipe smoking, and gifts, establishing a preliminary level of friendship according to the traditional rules of Indian etiquette. The Europeans liked to think that these flowery speeches and elaborate gestures of friendship constituted formal and exclusive alliances, but the Indians intended nothing beyond courtesy. The next day, the actual trading could begin.

The Europeans' exclusive emphasis on prime winter beaver, along with the Indians' increasing dependence on trade goods, meant that a family group that suffered a bad winter hunt faced disaster. There was nothing they could hunt in the summertime that was worth anything in trade, and without trade goods, they might be unable to survive another winter. Bands that found themselves in this predicament demanded credit. Although the Europeans were reluctant to extend it, they discovered that they had to do so in order to keep their clients from starving to death or seeking out rival traders for help.

While some Indians developed a loyalty to the French and others to the English, they were always alert to the possibility of a better deal and continuously played one side against the other. One particularly notorious bargainer was a Cree named Esquawino. An English trader at Moose Factory on James Bay admiringly described him as the "grand politician of all, being a free agent traveling about, sometimes to the French, at others to Albany and this fort, never drinks but has always his senses about him and makes the best of his market at all places."

In the area of most intense competition, the headwaters of the rivers that flowed eastward into the Saint Lawrence and those draining into James Bay, the beaver were soon trapped out. The main thrust of the fur

Animals adorn a birch-bark container, made by a Cree artisan about 1900. The Indians fashioned the receptacles by cutting a sheet of bark to a pattern, folding it to shape, and sewing it with spruce root. If the containers were designed to hold liquids, the seams were sealed with pitch.

trade moved westward, leaving the East Cree behind and engaging the West Cree, the Northern Ojibwa, and the Chipewyan.

Now it was not only the French and English who competed for trade. The West Cree adapted quickly to life in the fur trade—and to life with firearms. By the latter decades of the 17th century, the Hudson's Bay Company alone was trading as many as 500 guns and as much as 20,000 pounds of powder and shot in a single bartering season. The majority of these weapons went to the Cree, who used them to intimidate the Chipewyan Indians to their north living on lands that are today part of the Northwest Territories. The Cree so intimidated the Chipewyan that they stopped attempting to reach the Hudson's Bay Company posts with their superior stocks of beaver pelts, and instead traded them to the Cree, who then were able to make substantial profits at both ends of the pipeline.

After the French ceded all rights to the Hudson Bay territory (in the 1713 Treaty of Utrecht), the new governor of York Factory, James Knight, was determined not only to expand the Hudson's Bay Company's trade in the area, but to extend it to the Chipewyan. He learned of their desire to trade and their fear of Cree guns from some of their women who had been taken as slaves by Crees. He decided to build a post farther north, at the mouth of the Churchill River, to give the Chipewyan bands easier access to the British without having to run the Cree gantlet. But first, in 1715, Knight undertook to bring about peace between the groups, and gained as an ally in this enterprise a remarkable Chipewyan woman named Thanadelthur.

Thanadelthur had been captured by Crees, but managed to escape with another Chipewyan woman. The pair tried to make their way back to their people, surviving on whatever small game they could catch in their snares. Thanadelthur's companion died along the way, but somehow, Thanadelthur kept going until she stumbled across some English hunters

Ice and snow cover the ruins of Fort Prince of Wales, once a Hudson's Bay Company strong- hold at the mouth of the Churchill River in northern Manito- ba. The stone struc- ture replaced the wooden Fort Church- ill in 1733. Today the nearby town of Churchill is a major grain-shipping port.

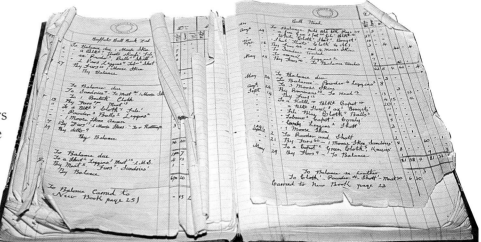

from York Factory. The hunters brought her into camp, where she soon recovered. Knight was instantly impressed with her extraordinary vivacity. Subsequently, when Knight persuaded a party of Crees to set out on a peacemaking mission to the Chipewyan bands, he sent Thanadelthur along to serve as an interpreter, with further instructions to tell her people "what commodities we deal for, and what seasons they must get their skins in, and how they must dress them and stretch them."

The well-thumbed pages of a 19th-century Hudson's Bay Company order book reveal the running accounts of two Indians, named Buffalo Bull Back Fat and Bull Head.

Thanadelthur, by the account of William Stuart, a company agent who accompanied the mission, soon became its "chief promoter and actor." The party ran out of food while trekking across a desolate stretch of terrain known as the Barren Grounds and was forced to split up. When the handful of remaining Crees refused to go deeper into Chipewyan territory for fear they would be killed, Thanadelthur persuaded Stuart and the Crees to give her 10 days to find her people and bring them to a peace conference. Traveling alone, she pressed on until she contacted a band of several hundred Chipewyans. She brought them into the Cree camp and persuaded them, through the sheer power of her personality, not to seek revenge on the small Cree delegation but to make peace. "She made them all stand in fear of her," recalled Stuart; "she scolded at some and [by] pushing of others, forced them to the peace."

Thanadelthur returned to York Factory with some of her people and reported to Knight in great detail on the prospects for the fur trade among the Chipewyan. In addition, she spoke of rich deposits of gold and copper farther to the northwest. But then, while planning with Knight another expedition to Chipewyan territory to complete plans for the new fort, she took sick and died. Knight was devastated. "She was," he wrote, "one of a very high spirit and of the firmest resolution that ever I see any body in my days."

Knight's astonishment at Thanadelthur's abilities reflected the fact that her physical and psychological strength did not conform to some European notions of femininity. Many of the traders were especially shocked to see the subarctic Indian woman's heavy burden of work—the Scottish fur trader and explorer Alexander Mackenzie called it "an uninterrupted succession of toil and pain." The trader David Thompson once saw a Chipewyan woman hauling an overloaded sled and sent one of his strongest men to relieve her. To Thompson's amazement, the man could barely move the load. The Chipewyan people themselves took pride in their women's physical prowess and indeed expected it. "Women were made for labor," a Chipewyan man told the English. "One of them can carry, or haul, as much as two men can."

Some Europeans also professed shock at Indian mores. Although youngsters were allowed a high degree of sexual freedom, marriages were usually arranged by family elders. Divorce was easily accomplished by either party and free of public censure, unless the couple had children. Polygamy and wife lending were common, especially among the western Indians. The Chipewyan were fond of wrestling matches, with the loser yielding his wife to the winner. But such behavior was always done within prescribed rules, as eight Frenchmen discovered when they attempted to sidestep Indian custom and force some Cree women to have sex with them in their trading post. The husbands and relatives of the women broke into the trading post and killed the French traders. An experienced coureur de bois explained that "you could lose your head if you take a young woman in this country without the consent of her parents."

Marriages between white traders and Indian women became common. The Indians saw marriage as a social and economic tool, and as a matter of course offered their female relatives in marriage as a way of cementing trade relations. Despite the denunciations of the Jesuits, French traders (and later the British) eagerly accepted Indian brides from virtually every subarctic group. Many of these marriages *à la façon du pays,* or "after the manner of the country," as the French phrase put it, proved to be stable unions characterized by great loyalty and affection. "There is indeed no living with comfort in this country until a person had forgot the great world and has his tastes and character formed on the current standard of the stage," wrote one trader, describing the joys of marriage to an Indian woman. "To any other being the vapid monotony of an inland trading post would be perfectly insufferable, while habit makes it familiar to us, softened as it is by the many tender ties which find a way to the heart."

The Indians imposed their customs on the process. A trader wishing to marry had to obtain the permission of the girl's parents, pay a bride price set by her relatives, and have a ceremonial smoke with the family elders. Then, perhaps after a brief public ceremony consisting mainly of a lecture to the bride on her future behavior, the couple took up their life together.

Such marriages were often ended not by death or divorce, but by retirement. When the husband's tenure as voyageur, or trader, was over, in

Indians swathed in Hudson's Bay blankets examine goods at a trading post in this 1881 sketch (top). The photograph shows a replica of a 19th-century fur-trading post at Rocky Mountain House National Historic Park in Alberta.

most cases he returned to his country, and the Indian woman and their children returned to her family. A number of traders made some provision for their Indian wives and children in their wills, and a few chose to stay in Canada and live by trapping and hunting.

This practice was forbidden by the Hudson's Bay Company. Those men who defied company policy were called "freemen." And after a difficult and embarrassing situation that arose in 1750, when for the first time a chief factor brought an Indian wife and mixed-blood baby back home with him and then died, the Hudson's Bay Company refused to transport Indians or mixed-bloods back to England.

One result of these "after the manner of the country" marriages, of course, was a growing number of half-white, half-Indian children, or Métis, as they were known. Although their upbringing sometimes caused stress between their parents—as when the European fathers exerted their patriarchal authority or sent the children away to be formally educated—their racial status was more advantage than disadvantage so long as the fur trade flourished. Métis girls were regarded as ideal wives, and the boys were thought to be exceptionally well set up for the trader's life. Many Indians believed that having parents from different cultures endowed the children with superior physical attributes for hunting and fighting.

With the assistance of another Chipewyan woman, James Knight constructed the Churchill River trading post in 1718. Although he died two years afterward, the trade he opened with the Chipewyan Indians at Fort Churchill prospered, without diminishing the volume at York Factory. Although the Cree resented the British for excluding them from trading at Fort Churchill in favor of the Chipewyan, an uneasy peace prevailed for much of the time.

The Cree were still active elsewhere. In the early decades of the 18th century, they pushed out to the southwest in order to open a trade in furs with the Plains Indians—the Lakota and the Blackfeet—who could not participate in the trade directly because they did not use canoes. Many Crees spent the winter with the Plains Indians, trapping and trading for beaver and hunting bison, then traveled downriver to Hudson Bay in the spring. And during this period, the Chipewyan Indians began to take up the role of middlemen between the English and the more distant Yellowknife, Dogrib, and Slavey people.

These trade items are representative of the types of goods commonly swapped for furs: a Hudson's Bay Company-style ax; a man's ring; calico cloth; and a Chief Blanket with multicolored borders and four "points," or bars, at the edge, indicating that it weighs six pounds and measures 72 by 90 inches.

The British clung to their sedentary ways—waiting at their posts for the Indians to come to them—and, as a result, remained vulnerable to competition from the coureurs de bois. Cut off by treaty from Hudson Bay, the French pushed westward and, by the 1740s, had reached Lake Winnipeg and the Saskatchewan River and had begun to draw off the inland trade from the Hudson's Bay Company. They also moved as close as they could to the James Bay posts, with which they competed by cutting the prices of their trade goods.

This new French advance into the interior was doomed, however, by the French and Indian War of the 1750s. During this final contest between France and Great Britain for supremacy on the American continent, Britain's dominance of the seas severely constrained the French fur trade. With the fall of Quebec and Montreal, French domination of the Saint Lawrence fur-trading network ended. But independent British traders took up where the French had left off, quickly learning the French methods and employing the services of the coureurs de bois, who still lived in the wilderness as French Canadians.

Within a few years, the Hudson's Bay Company was once again facing vigorous competition of the same kind it had experienced before England won the war—now from people it referred to contemptuously as "pedlars from Quebec." At long last, the company abandoned its policy of requiring the Indians to travel to its shoreline forts and began building trading posts in the interior. Until now, its only inland fort was Henley House, built on the Albany River in 1720 as a way station for Indians traveling to a Hudson's Bay Company shoreline post. Now the company began constructing a series of inland trading posts, beginning with the Cumberland House, on the Saskatchewan River above Lake Winnipeg.

As the fur trade rippled westward, it continued to shape Indian life in an inexorable pattern. In 1770 Hudson's Bay Company agent Samuel Hearne, accompanied by the Chipewyan leader Matonabbee, traveled the country northwest of Lake Athabaska and confirmed that the Chipewyan were doing to the Dogrib and Yellowknife exactly what the Cree had once done to them: charging them exorbitant prices for trade goods and preventing them from establishing their own trade relations with the English. "It is a political scheme of our northern [Chipewyan] traders to prevent

THE ARTISTRY OF THE WOMEN

Since early times, subarctic Indian women have employed porcupine quills, along with sinew, to produce decorative embroidery on animal hides. During the long, cold winters, or while in menstrual seclusion, they completed many magnificent pieces of handiwork for their families. Traditional design repertoires expanded in the 19th century when nuns and teachers introduced European materials, techniques, and floral designs. The resulting blend of Indian and Western art forms was perfected by the Athapaskan women.

As part of the fur trade, Europeans offered beads, fabrics, thread, and sewing needles in barter. According to Hudson's Bay Company chief factor Alexander Murray, "Without beads and plenty of them you can do little or no good here." By the end of the 19th century, beaded floral design had become prevalent across most of central and western Canada, as well as in parts of Alaska, and regional design variations had developed. Porcupine quillwork continued only occasionally.

In addition to clothing and other accessories, the women decorated a variety of containers. These included game-bags made of netting to let in fresh air; firebags to carry such items as a flint-and-steel for starting fires, shot for guns, or tobacco; various types of knife sheaths; and moss bags to carry infants, diapered with absorbent sphagnum.

Traditions of Athapaskan ornamentation have continued into modern times. Today Athapaskan women fashion fine embroidery items to sell to the public, but on those occasions when they wish to honor someone with a special gift, they still turn to embroidery.

A Slavey woman selects beads that she will thread and embroider onto a patterned base. The pelican pouch at right was used by a Chipewyan woman to store her embroidery equipment. Pelicans are still found on the lakes of Canada's Prairie Provinces.

HUNTING SHIRT, UPPER YUKON RIVER REGION

SMOKING CAP, GREAT SLAVE LAKE-MACKENZIE RIVER REGION

GAUNTLETS, HAN

MOCCASINS, DOGRIB

DRESS, FORT CHIPEWYAN REGION

GAMEBAG, DOGRIB

FIREBAG, SEKANI

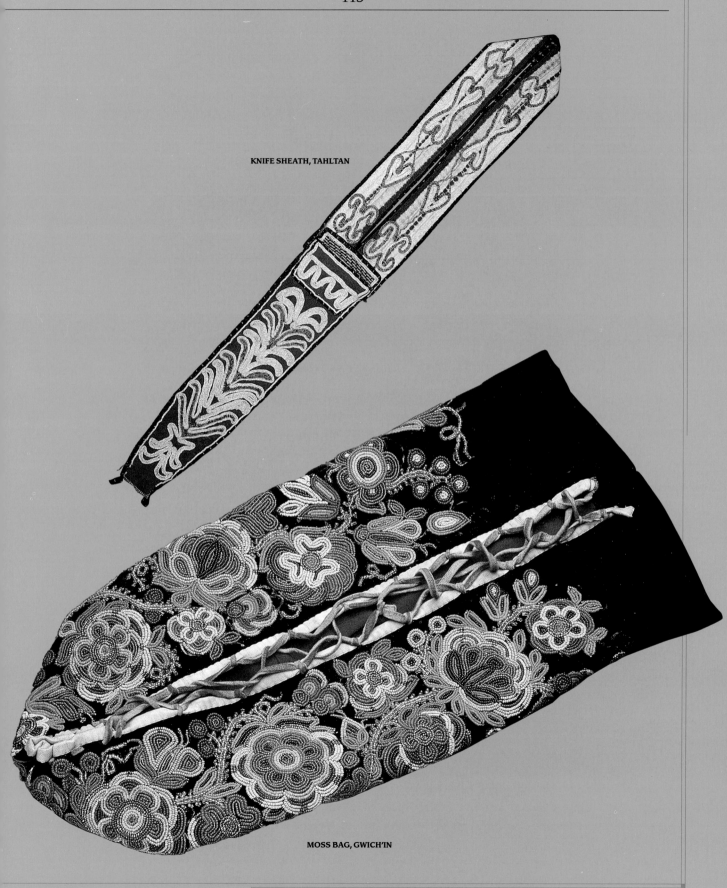

KNIFE SHEATH, TAHLTAN

MOSS BAG, GWICH'IN

such an intercourse," Hearne reported, "as it would greatly lessen their consequence and emolument." When urged to come to Fort Churchill to trade, the Dogrib responded that "not one out of three that have undertaken the journey have ever lived to return."

As had been the case so frequently in the past, a great many more Indians were dying from diseases than from any hostile action. Once a native population came in contact with the Europeans, the ravages of disease became constant, and there were exceptionally deadly outbreaks of influenza in the late 1740s and of smallpox in the 1780s. The latter epidemic swept across a major portion of the continent, devastating Cree, Assiniboin, Northern Ojibwa, and Chipewyan populations.

Like the Montagnais before them, the Cree found that once the fur trade had moved on, they were less able to provide for themselves, even though they continued to hunt and trap. Some of them chose to accompany the traders westward, acting as guides, interpreters, and laborers. But a large number of them were reduced to a state of dependence on the supply posts left in the traders' wake, acting as hunters and provisioners when possible, but often dependent on charity.

As the fur trade shifted ever farther westward, the Hudson's Bay Company as well as the independent traders had to deal with a progressively more difficult logistical problem—sustaining the traders while they were transporting goods and furs. This was a problem especially for the French and their successors, because their trade involved long and arduous canoe trips and tight schedules. Stopping frequently along the way to hunt

Cree hunters paddle into deeper water before starting up their outboard motors to head off into James Bay on a fall goose hunt. Each autumn, hundreds of thousands of geese gather at the bay on their annual migration to the United States.

game to eat required too much time. Nor was it practicable to transport bulky or heavy supplies; cargo space was limited and had to be devoted almost exclusively to the trade.

The new answer to the dilemma was found in the form of pemmican, a term derived from Indian words for "meat" and "fat." It was actually a means of preserving meat by slicing it thin, drying it thoroughly, pounding it into shreds, and then mixing it with melted animal fat. Properly prepared and sealed with tallow in a rawhide container, pemmican could remain edible for decades. Preparing it, however, was not easy, and finding supplies of pemmican became a major problem for the traders.

Hoping to attract a flock of geese within shotgun range, a Cree hunter prepares to prop up the head of a dead goose on a stick in a "feeding ground" composed entirely of dead geese. The Cree also use handmade decoys made of twigs (inset).

A Cree hunter heads for home with the pair of Canada geese he has shot slung over his shoulder. If the birds are not eaten immediately, they will be stored for the winter.

Another problem for the individual traders was a lack of capital. The constraints of independent action became more and more apparent, until one of the increasing number of Scotsmen who were emigrating to Canada to take part in this trade—one Simon McTavish—proposed the answer. In 1783 McTavish and a group of partners organized the North West Company, which united most of the independent traders and posed a formidable new threat to the Hudson's Bay Company.

The North West Company established trading posts on Lake Athabaska and Great Slave Lake, from whence they pushed into the country of the Yellowknife, Dogrib, and Slavey people to the west and north. Forced to respond to this encroachment on their trading territory, the Hudson's Bay Company established its own forts on both lakes and sent its own traders out to get the trade back. While the traders of both companies demanded loyalty and more beaver, the aggressive Crees who went with them virtu-

A Cree woman prepares geese for cooking while others, suspended from hooks in the rafters of the "meechwap," or cooking lodge, roast over a log fire. She will use fat drippings collected in the frying pans to baste the birds.

ally went to war, driving the Beaver and Slavey Indians north and west, even while trading with them at considerable profit. At the outset of their competition, the North West Company shipped four times as many furs to Britain as did the Hudson's Bay Company.

The Hudson's Bay Company had suffered a severe setback in 1782 when a French force allied with the rebellious American colonies destroyed Fort Prince of Wales (formerly known as Fort Churchill) and York Factory. It took four years for the company to recover and resume its expansion on the North and South Saskatchewan Rivers. By that time, they discovered that the North West Company had moved far beyond them. In 1787 the North West Company established Fort Chipewyan on Lake Athabaska (in what later became northeastern Alberta). Two years later, the founder of that fort, 25-year-old Scotsman Alexander Mackenzie, pushed northward past Great Slave Lake down a broad river—later given his name—to the Arctic Ocean. And four years after that, he explored the Peace River and its tributaries westward to the Pacific, opening to the North West Company yet another avenue to fresh supplies of furs.

Competition for the fur trade intensified further, not only between the two principal companies but also among them and various smaller enterprises, including a coalition that was led by Alexander Mackenzie called the XY Company. Trading posts in the Athabaska country proliferated, with each company recruiting help from among the resident Indians.

The rival Europeans demanded of their Indian partners unconditional loyalty, a concept the Yellowknife found as difficult to grasp as had the Cree and the Montagnais before them. In this instance, the standard remedy of appointing a captain did not work. As one frustrated trader explained, "None of their principal men can have sufficient authority." The traders began appointing Chipewyans to captain Yellowknife trapping parties. In fact, some trapping parties had more than one captain, each acting on behalf of a different company.

As before, the more intense the competition among Europeans, the greater the Indians' purchasing power. But competition also had its corrosive side. The traders plied the bands with gifts and liquor—shipping records indicate that consumption of alcohol in the Canadian Northwest doubled at the turn of the 19th century. Sometimes, the traders abused the Indians for real or imagined disloyalty. And as they bustled among the bands in search of furs, they accidentally spread killer diseases.

"Indolence, robbery, and murder are the consequences of an opposition in trade," wrote a North West Company trader named Willard Ferdinand Wentzel in 1807. "It destroys trade, creates vice, and renders people crafty, ruins good morals, and almost totally abolishes every humane sentiment in both Christian and Indian breast."

The Beaver Indians, having been attacked by Crees and Chipewyans in the employ of traders, and suffering from sickness and alcohol abuse,

The Dogrib protected bundles of food from animals by hanging them from tripods of saplings like this one, photographed in 1925 near Great Slave Lake, Northwest Territories.

A cabin cache built on legs to discourage wolves and other meat eaters stands in ruins near the deserted Tanana village of Coschacket in central Alaska. In 1958, the Indians moved to a better site on the Yukon River.

became disgusted with the trading competition and hostile to all intruders. Many Chipewyans abandoned the fur trade and returned to their nomadic, caribou-centered life.

The death and disaffection of the Indians, along with the depletion of the beaver and the saturation of the home markets, all took their toll. Everyone's profits were declining, and soon all involved in the fur trade could see that changes had to be made. On March 26, 1821, the North West Company and the Hudson's Bay Company ended their fratricidal competition and joined forces. Now, virtually all of the Indians of the Canadian Northwest, their bands scattered and depleted, uprooted, and divided against one another, would be dealing with a single monolithic source of trade goods. Few of them were left in the role of middlemen; even fewer were capable of returning to the old ways of self-reliance. ◆

ALLIANCE OF TWO BLOODS

"Our young men will marry your daughters, and we will be one people." This promise, which was made by the 17th-century French explorer Samuel de Champlain to tribal leaders he met with in eastern Canada, was fulfilled in the Métis—a distinctive people of mixed Indian and European ancestry. As Champlain foresaw, many Frenchmen who ventured into the northern forest as fur traders took native wives, often Cree or Ojibwa, and their children inherited the traditions of both parents. These Métis evolved their own way of speaking, combining French with Algonquian terms. Over the years, the cultural mix became even richer, as English traders intermarried with the Métis or with members of various northern peoples, whose offspring often became part of the Métis community.

Most early marriages between white fur traders and Indian women took place after the custom of the country, that is, without the blessing of the church. Nevertheless, they were strong alliances that conferred benefits on both sides. The woman brought into the community a trading partner who could supply the Indians with European goods. The man gained a wife who knew the country and could help him prepare his furs—and whose male kin were often expert trappers.

As future generations of Métis grew up around the trading posts, they came to play a vital role there as intermediaries between Indians and Europeans, serving the fur companies as translators, mail clerks, and officials. Other Métis ranged far afield as trappers, traders, and freighters—hardy men who hauled the goods. Many supplemented what they earned through the fur trade by joining in seasonal buffalo hunts on the northern Plains and selling the preserved meat at towns and trading posts.

Unlike people of mixed ancestry living elsewhere in North America, who became part of either Indian or white society, the Métis remained a distinct group. Long ignored by the Canadian government, they fought many a battle against authorities during the 19th century and endured defeat and displacement. Ultimately, however, they were able to achieve success in gaining rights and recognition as a people and in preserving their unique culture.

The handwoven Assomption sash (top), so called for the Quebec town where many were made, became a trademark of the Métis, as shown by the freighters above, at a portage on the Athabaska River in Alberta in 1899.

Métis Catherine Lafferty sits with her children James and Edward at Fort Resolution on Great Slave Lake in 1912. The elaborate floral beadwork on the moss bag swaddling her infant typifies the mingling of European designs with Indian patterns in Métis handicrafts.

BACK COUNTRY TRAVELERS

Whether as independent operators or as company employees, the Métis were the mainstay of the fur trade. Covering vast distances in a variety of vehicles, they conveyed their own goods—or the company's wares—between the back country and the trading posts. Early on, they relied primarily on canoes, which they paddled or portaged from one body of water to another. But as trade routes expanded, they turned to other modes of transportation—scows, for travel downriver; dogsleds, for snow and ice; and carts, used mainly to haul buffalo meat across the prairie. They devised their own cart for that purpose, named for Manitoba's Red River valley, where many Métis lived and launched their hunting forays. A creaky vehicle with an ungreased wooden axle, the Red River cart announced their approach miles in advance. Impressed, the Cree referred to the Métis by a term meaning "half man-half wagon."

A mid-19th-century painting by Canadian Paul Kane reveals the care the Métis took in decorating their sleds—and gear for their dogs like the embroidered saddle blanket above.

Pausing for a smoke, Métis lounge beside their Red River cart in Manitoba about 1860. In earlier days, Métis canoemen stopped to smoke with such regularity that they measured distances in pipes.

Rivermen ease a large flat-bottomed scow over the Big Cascade of the Athabaska River in Alberta. Newly built each spring, scows made one trip downstream and were then broken up.

IN PURSUIT OF THE BUFFALO

Many Métis living near the eastern edge of the Plains in the 18th and 19th centuries took part in buffalo hunts twice a year. Each spring and fall, hundreds of Red River carts, carrying entire Métis families, set off for the hunting grounds. By 1840 the number of carts departing from settlements along the Red River surpassed 1,000.

The buffalo hunt was governed by strict rules that were designed to maintain order in camp. But while the Métis kept peace among themselves, they sometimes had to draw on their skills as riders and marksmen to fight off resentful bands of Sioux.

After the buffalo were killed, the women mixed the dried meat with fat and berries. This durable pemmican was then sold to fur companies, who used it to provision their far-ranging traders. The hunts proved rewarding in more ways than one: They were festive occasions that brought Métis together from scattered communities.

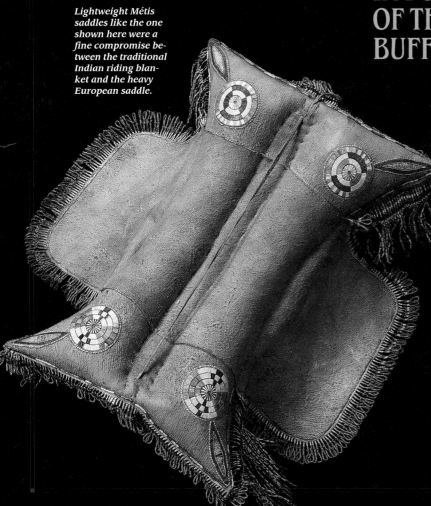

Lightweight Métis saddles like the one shown here were a fine compromise between the traditional Indian riding blanket and the heavy European saddle.

Red River carts sit alongside tipis at a Métis hunting camp on the Plains in 1874. After the buffalo hunt, people loaded these carts with pemmican; the dried meat was lighter and easier to transport than fresh meat.

Métis horsemen chase down buffalo in this painting by Paul Kane. To mark his kill, a hunter dropped a strip of cloth with his insignia on it beside the buffalo he felled.

Three women wearing tartan shawls of the sort favored by the Métis pose at a hunting camp about 1900. The shawls were trade goods, obtained in part with proceeds from the sale of pemmican the women prepared.

A spirited couple dance to the tune of fiddles at a Red River settlement in this engraving from the 1860s. As performed by the Métis, such jigs had a strong Indian beat.

Chokecherries like those pictured in this sketch were gathered by Métis women and used to flavor pemmican.

THE PLIGHT OF THE DEFEATED

Unrecognized by the Canadian government as either Indian or white, the Métis were denied a territory of their own and public benefits such as education. Intent on redressing their grievances, they rose up in a series of rebellions that were led by Louis Riel beginning in 1869. The bitter struggle ended with their defeat in 1885.

Afterward, many Métis fled their homes along the Red River and the Saskatchewan River in the face of a rising tide of white settlement. Most of them moved northwestward into more remote areas—upper Saskatchewan and Alberta, the Mackenzie District of the Northwest Territories, and the Yukon. Others turned south into the United States, eventually settling with Ojibwas at the Turtle Mountain Reservation in North Dakota.

The plight of the Métis was compounded by the decline of the fur trade and the virtual disappearance of the buffalo. Faced with dislocation and the collapse of their traditional economy, they struggled to find new ways to support themselves and their families.

This Métis trapper, pictured in the 1930s with his dog and gun, was among those who continued to derive some income from the dwindling fur trade. Trappers supplemented their take by hunting with rifles like the Winchester above—carried in a buckskin sheath.

With the advent of steam power, Métis abandoned their scows and served as crewmen or captains on vessels like the "Distributor"—shown here in 1918. At the time, it was the largest steamer operating on the Mackenzie River.

Still relying on horse power in 1942, a farmer turns the soil at a Métis community in northern Alberta. Often working poor land with outmoded equipment, few Métis succeeded as farmers.

Métis women from Green Lake, Saskatchewan, embroider moccasins for market. Such beadwork skills and designs have been passed down from mother to daughter over the generations.

Using modern equipment, Métis living in northern Saskatchewan earn extra income harvesting wild rice, a traditional activity rooted in the Cree and Ojibwa heritage of many Métis.

ECHOES OF THE PAST

Once called Canada's forgotten people, the Métis have at last been acknowledged. In 1938 they received territory of their own in Alberta with the passage of the Métis Betterment Act. In 1980 they were recognized by the Canadian government as an aboriginal people and thus became eligible for the rights and services extended to other native groups. They are still waging some hard battles—but only in court over issues of land and mineral rights.

Many Métis live and work today in ways that echo their past. Hunting, gathering, and the lively crafts of embroidery and music making remain important to them as pastimes—and often as means of subsistence. Few of them are rich in possessions. But as the Cree said of them admiringly in the past, the proud Métis are "their own bosses."

Brothers Frank and Robert Pruden skin a moose beside Crooked Lake on the Kikino settlement, one of several areas reserved for the Métis in Alberta.

Fred Allery of the Métis community at North Dakota's Turtle Mountain Reservation rests with his fiddle between dances. Métis fiddle music combines old French jigs with Indian drum rhythms.

3

A smiling hunter carries home the antlers and hide of a caribou. The large, deerlike animals provided northern Athapaskans with most of the necessities of life—including weapons, like the antler club shown above, left.

RESHAPING THE INDIAN'S WORLD

"My grandfather, he was some kind of prophet!" exclaimed Jeremy Caribou, a Missinipi Cree from west-central Manitoba. One day in the 1930s when Caribou was a child, his grandfather, a respected medicine man named Antoine Dumas, hunkered down next to the family fireplace and divined the future for his grandson. Dumas derived his insights in the traditional Cree manner—from his dreams. "You're going to see a lot of things in your later life," the old man told the child. "But now you're just a little boy. You know nothing. You have no knowledge of what's to become of you later."

Caribou remembered how his grandfather turned first in the direction of the west. "Water problems," the old man said grimly. "That water is not going to supply you all your life. There's white men over there that plugged up the water. They're fooling around with that water." Next, Caribou's grandfather cast his gaze to the north. He saw more white men. "They're over there again," he said. "They're there ahead of you. They're digging holes in the ground. And they're taking money from the ground. And they got these big *miskanaw* [a Cree word for trail]. And they're hiding that money all over the north from you. And then they have a snake passing, crawling through your land. Right by your reserve there's some kind of a snake."

Looking to the east, the old man saw more threatened land. "It doesn't look too good," he cautioned. Finally, he faced the south. "There's lots of white people coming," he warned. "And they'll bring a lot of things that are both good and bad for the people of the north. And the people are going to try to live with them, alongside them."

Decades later, Caribou reflected on his grandfather's words and marveled at their accuracy. Large numbers of whites had indeed settled on Cree lands, just as his grandfather had predicted. Caribou realized that many of his grandfather's prophecies referred to the infrastructure and development of modern Canada: Giant hydroelectric dams had altered the flow of rivers; the big miskanaw his grandfather had seen were asphalt highways; the holes in the ground, mines; and the snake, railroads.

A group of Dogrib Indians unload their canoes at Fort Resolution, along the shore of Great Slave Lake, in this 1901 photograph. Lodgepoles, blankets, bark strips, and bales of furs are crowded about the landing site.

A Cree family paddles supplies and equipment across a lake in northern Quebec. Although most modern-day Crees have permanent homes located in villages, many of them still go into the bush to hunt each fall, returning home in the spring.

"He was right," Caribou concluded. "All these things that the old man told me were going to involve my life, they're accurate so far. He even told me about the [atomic] bomb. And that I'm going to see jets flying overhead going faster than lightning and sounding like thunder. But then I was a boy. I never knew those things would exist."

Antoine Dumas had experienced great changes himself. When he was a little boy, Canada had become a self-governing dominion. One of the first actions of the new government was to negotiate a series of treaties that moved many subarctic Indians, including Dumas's own family, onto reservations, or reserves, as the Canadians call them. Those Indians who did not live on reserves gave up their old nomadic ways for more settled lives in small, log-cabin hamlets that were located close to trading posts, Christian missions, schools, and nursing stations—changes brought about in large part by the merger of the two great fur-trading giants, the upstart North West Company and the old established Hudson's Bay Company.

When Sir George Simpson, first governor of the newly consolidated Hudson's Bay Company, surveyed his domain in 1821, he realized that even as the eastern trade continued, the future of the business lay to the west of Hudson Bay, where fresh sources of furs were plentiful and new groups of Indians were eager to trade. As his first order of business, Simpson launched a series of reforms to put the fur trade on sounder economic footing. He shut down competing and unprofitable trading posts, reorganized the procurement of supplies, redrew trading territories, and began the policy of "allotting certain tracts of the country to the different bands."

Simpson's measures benefited company shareholders but brought hardship to many subarctic Indians. Where the competition for furs had been most intense—the Peace River west of Lake Athabaska and the Mackenzie River system northwest of Great Slave Lake—bands that had come to depend on specific traders and forts for their livelihood found themselves suddenly abandoned. In some cases, their desperation turned to violence. Company men were killed, and two posts had to be evacuated in the Peace River country in the aftermath of reorganization.

The effects of the new monopoly on the Mackenzie River valley Indians were typical. In 1822 the Hudson's Bay Company took over Fort of the Forks, built two years earlier by the North West Company on an island at the confluence of the Liard and Mackenzie Rivers. It was renamed Fort Simpson and designated the depot and administrative center for the region. The Hudson's Bay Company's original post in the region, Fort Liard,

built about 1800 on the Liard near the Black River, became strictly a provisioning center for Fort Simpson's personnel. The Slavey, Dogrib, Beaver, and Sekani bands that had formerly traded with both the North West Company and the Hudson's Bay Company now had to deal exclusively with Fort Simpson. The following year, Fort Good Hope, originally the most northerly post of the North West Company, was moved 100 miles upstream from its location on Manitou Island in the Mackenzie, and from then on, all the Indians of the Mackenzie River valley were obliged to trade directly with those two posts.

The new policy disrupted well-established patterns of movement. Quarrels broke out when bands of Dogrib, Hare, and Slavey Indians moved into the caribou-rich lands between Great Slave and Great Bear Lakes and north to Muskox Lake, the traditional hunting grounds of the Yellowknife Indians. The Yellowknife, led by a warrior named Akaitcho, began to tyrannize the intruders, robbing them and kidnapping their women and children. During the winter of 1823, the Dogrib, Hare, and Slavey struck back, murdering an entire encampment of 34 of their tormentors—perhaps 20 percent of the entire Yellowknife population.

The most populous of the northern Athapaskan groups were the Chipewyan, whose extensive territory to the east of Mackenzie District included the transition zone between boreal forest and the tundra of the Barren Grounds. Throughout the 1820s, the Chipewyan were the cause of friction with other Indian groups as they struggled to maintain a viable role for themselves in the fur trade. They insisted, sometimes violently, on

A Chipewyan woman and child set out to hunt muskrat along the shallow margins of Garson Lake in western Saskatchewan. The small aquatic mammal has always been a significant source of food as well as fur for many subarctic Indians.

A Cree woman hangs marten (smaller) and otter pelts stretched over wooden frames on a crossbar to dry in the cold air. Trapped throughout the winter, marten have always been a major commercial resource for the Indians.

being middlemen where none were needed; on directing the trapping activities of other bands, as they had done in the past; and on trapping in the territories of other bands.

Eventually, however, a quieter routine emerged. Each band became associated with one particular trading post and incorporated it into their seasonal movements. They gathered at the post in summer and made it the site of their annual ceremonies and celebrations. At the onset of winter, they headed back into their hunting grounds, with provisions and equipment obtained on credit from the fort, for a winter of hunting, fishing, and trapping. In January, and again in April, they returned to the post to pay off their debts with furs and to resupply, moving back to the fort again after the breakup of the winter ice.

The new routine forced many subarctic Indians into a pattern of ever-increasing dependency, not only for trade goods but also for credit, and

sometimes even for food. The higher price of trade goods caused some groups to allocate more time to trapping beaver and other furbearers, reducing the time they could devote to hunting. As a result, there was frequently a greater reliance on small game and fish for subsistence. Eating and hunting habits began to change, along with notions of land use. The communal sharing of wide expanses and plentiful resources slowly gave way to individual claims by extended families, especially among the Algonquian-speaking peoples of the East.

In the early 1830s, the living conditions of the Indians worsened dramatically. By that time, the snowshoe hare had become a principal source of food. For reasons that are not fully understood, the hare population waxes and wanes in six-to-14-year cycles, and in the fall of 1830, it collapsed. With no hare to trap and few alternate sources of food, the Indians suffered widespread starvation. One entire band of Chipewyans, 40 in number, died of hunger near Fort Liard.

Warfare erupted as the Dogrib and Slavey pushed northward, intruding on Yellowknife territory in the pursuit of caribou. The search for food became so desperate that there was little time available for trapping beaver. Wretched bands of starving Indians overwhelmed the trading posts, begging for food. In the spring of 1832, a Hudson's Bay Company official observed that "I seldom have witnessed for a whole season such a continued stress for provisions for immediate consumption."

Four women dress a moose skin stretched tightly across a log frame. After fleshing it, they will tan the hide, making it soft and pliable by soaking it and rubbing it with a paste made of water and moose brains, followed by extensive stretching. If brown is the desired color, the moose leather will then be smoked over a smudge fire.

Age-old Indian mourning rituals sometimes made conditions worse. When an Indian died, his relatives not only buried his clothing and equipment with him but also destroyed or gave away their own most prized possessions as a gesture of sympathy and grief. As death from the famine became widespread, grief-stricken families sometimes deprived themselves of the guns, traps, snowshoes, and other tools their survival required.

In 1833 the Hudson's Bay Company announced several new policies designed to stimulate trade and increase profits. Having reduced the number of posts, the company set about reducing the overhead of those re-

Two Gwich'in women stand outside their lodge in the Yukon Territory. Apart from their expertise in making clothing and preparing savory food, subarctic women are famed for their skill at repairing equipment and snaring small game.

maining. It again cut the prices it would pay for furs and raised the prices of its trade goods. Giving less for each fur would bring in more furs—or so John Stuart, the company official in charge of Fort Liard, argued. "It is a mistaken idea that a high price will even induce the Indians to bring in a larger quantity, quite the reverse," Stuart explained to the traders. "They are naturally indolent, when they get their wants for little they will labor but little, and if they could get their wants for nothing they would do still less."

The company decided it would no longer recognize the rank of trading-post chief and trapping-party captain, positions it had created among the Indians. Now the company intended to deal directly with individual trappers and to force more Indians out into the country in search of beaver.

The most devastating policy shift, however, was the company's decision not to extend any more credit—an attempt at generating greater profits that experienced trappers knew would fail. "The Indian trade never was and never can be carried on to advantage where no debt is given," John Stuart declared, voicing the concern of the Mackenzie District traders, for it was "the supplies given in the fall on debt that enables them to hunt in winter." Many traders simply ignored the no-credit rule. Where it was applied, however, it only succeeded in imposing a further hardship on an already troubled people and contributed to a decline in trade. Two years later, the company was forced to reinstate some credit.

The company's officers in London believed that they could dictate the terms and conditions of the fur trade because of the Indians' increased dependency on the trading posts. In fact, however, the traders had become almost as dependent on the Indians as the Indians were on them. Although the posts often harbored supplies and provisions that became critical resources in times of famine, normally it was the Indians who supplied the meat, fish, waterfowl, and pemmican to feed the traders, clerks, and shippers of the trade.

Before the advent of the fur trade, the subarctic Indians of today's Northwest Territories, like their counterparts in the East, had rarely experienced widespread famine. The Chipewyan and Yellowknife bands had lived, the trader Samuel Hearne recorded in 1771, "generally in a state of plenty, without trouble of risk," along the northern edge of the forest and the southern edge of the tundra. They enjoyed an inexhaustible supply of caribou—estimated at two million strong before 1700—supplemented by vast numbers of fish, waterfowl, and small game. Farther south, beyond the migration routes of the caribou, the Slavey, Dogrib, Hare, Beaver, and Sekani bands had relied on large herds of wood bison, which, unlike the

A harvest of splayed salmon dries over a smoky fire at an Ahtna fishing camp on the Copper River in southeastern Alaska. The Ahtna bands divide the year among their fishing camps, up-land hunting camps, and winter houses.

Subarctic women have long done much of the fishing, using a variety of techniques that include angling, spearing, netting, and trapping in weirs like the one at left on the Slave River in the Northwest Territories. The Ahtna woman below is fishing for salmon with a dip net twined with spruce roots.

grazing plains bison, were browsers that flourished in the mixed-wood forests. Where neither caribou nor bison could be found, there were moose and deer. Hearne noted that the Indians were "seldom exposed to the gripping hand of famine, so frequently felt by those who are called the annual traders."

Amid such accessible plenty, and with the number of Indians relatively low, there had never been a need for conservation. Over millennia, Indian hunters had maintained a spiritual kinship with the big game animals that provided the means for their survival. Each hunt began with special ceremonies addressed to the animals' spiritual guardians. The hunters expressed their needs, professed their worthiness, asked for cooperation, and prayed for success. The Indians believed that if they demonstrated the proper attitude, the spirit guardians would allow them to harvest the animals in modest quantities. After making a kill, an Indian hunter was careful to show the carcass the greatest respect, often laying it out on a ceremonial blanket and making an offering of tobacco before carefully butchering it and disposing of the remains in ritually prescribed ways. If everyone lived according to tradition, the Indians thought that the animal populations would never be depleted.

Indian hunters believed that if an animal's spirit was displeased by the way it was treated, however, it might withhold future success, refusing to allow itself to be taken. And if the offense was great, the spirit guardian might retaliate with a terrible curse. In such a relationship, there was no place for excessive killing; but of course, the kinship between humans and animals had developed over many centuries when there had been no possible reason for harvesting more animals than were needed by the band for food, clothing, and shelter. But the advent of the fur trade, with its steel traps and guns and insatiable demand for pelts, imposed new conditions.

According to Governor Simpson of the Hudson's Bay Company, by 1820 there were no longer any bison within a week's travel of Fort Chipewyan. By 1889 only 550 wood bison could be counted anywhere in the region. Moose were hunted out from some areas before 1821. Caribou were steadily depleted throughout the 19th century. Even while struggling to maximize profits, the Hudson's Bay Company was forced to take conservation measures. In 1825 the company established a fixed trapping season. In 1830 it set game limits and, in 1833, imposed restrictions on beaver trapping while offering higher prices for other furbearing animals such as muskrat.

In the tapestry of death and destruction that characterized the fur trade during the 19th century, special afflictions were visited on a unique group of people spawned by the contact of the European and native cultures. The children of white fathers and Indian mothers, deprived of the full support of either culture, became the only northern group to rise against their

The daughter and granddaughter of an Ahtna woman named Katie John retrieve salmon from a pen where the fish have been stored after being caught in the nearby Copper River. A recent lawsuit by John forced the State of Alaska to recognize her family's right to fish in the river.

An Indian woman pours birch sap into a bucket while her son samples the raw liquid. Sap scrapers like the double-edged caribou antler above were used to collect the sticky liquid. Birch sap was boiled into syrup and mixed with dry fish meal for eating.

foreign oppressors. Called many things, these mixed-blood children came to be known best as Métis.

By the time of the consolidation of the North West Company and the Hudson's Bay Company, thousands of Métis were at work in the fur trade. The majority were French-speaking Catholics, but many were English-speaking Anglicans. Most of the men were adept at Indian hunting methods and preferred the freedom of Indian life to the strictures of white settlements. Still, while most worked as hunters and trappers, many others served the industry in other capacities, working as factors, clerks, guides, provisioners, packers, porters, and boatmen.

The various groups of Métis had little in common except what they were not: neither all Indian nor all white. As a 20th-century Métis leader said about his people, "They are Métis because they are not somebody else." That categorization notwithstanding, at the beginning of the 19th century, Métis composed the largest ethnic group in what are now the southern portions of Manitoba, Saskatchewan, and Alberta.

A Carrier woman uses a knife to scrape off the rough outer layer of a sheet of birch bark to make a basket. Before the arrival of the Europeans, the Indians removed sheets of bark with wooden tools, like the one above.

In 1811, a decade before his company's consolidation with the North West Company, Thomas Douglas, Earl of Selkirk, of the Hudson's Bay Company, established a farming settlement on 116,000 square miles of fertile land that stretched from Lake Winnipeg south 100 miles to the United States-Canada border. Called the Red River Colony, it included the confluence of the Red and Assiniboine Rivers in what is today the city of Winnipeg.

Lord Selkirk hoped the colony would provide retiring employees with an alternative to returning to England, thus keeping them and their sometimes substantial amounts of money in the country. He also hoped that it

would offer farming as an alternate method of subsistence to the Métis and demonstrate the benefits of a settled community.

The Red River Colony lay across the major North West Company trade route from the Great Lakes to the Lake Athabaska country. The North West Company assumed that since Lord Selkirk was a major shareholder in the rival Hudson's Bay Company, he intended to use the colony to restrict his competitors' access to prime furs. The North West Company therefore encouraged local Métis to regard the settlement as an incursion on their territory and a threat to their livelihood. The latter claim was given credibility when the Red River settlers blocked the North West Company's pemmican supply lines. The Métis organized an armed party to reopen the lines, the settlers marched out to meet them, and at the ensuing Battle of Seven Oaks, 22 settlers, including the governor of the Red River Colony, were killed with the loss of only one Métis.

After the 1821 merger, however, many hundreds of Métis were thrown out of work. "These people form a burden which cannot be got rid of without expense," wrote a Hudson's Bay Company manager early in 1822, "and, if allowed to remain in their present condition, will become dangerous to the peace of the country and the safety of the trading posts. We consider that all these people ought to be removed to Red River." There, he observed, they could be "civilized and instructed in religion."

The Hudson's Bay Company agreed and encouraged the Métis to settle down as farmers in the Red River Colony. Alexander Ross, a Scottish trader who moved to the colony to raise his Métis children, remembered that the company welcomed all Métis ready "to throw off your savage customs, follow the habits of white men, and cultivate civilization." But the welcome was accompanied by a warning: "There is no field here for the

THE RISING GENERATION

Subarctic Indian babies, like these infants from the Montreal River region in Ontario, are still trussed on cradleboards after first being comfortably diapered with absorbent moss and wrapped with soft materials, such as the skin of a caribou embryo or, in modern times, cotton cloth. The moss is collected from the forest floor (opposite).

pursuits of savage life; your hunting and roving propensities cannot be indulged; you must settle down, cultivate the soil, and become Christians."

By 1831 nearly 1,300 Métis had moved to the colony. That number would double in the succeeding decade and reach 12,000 by 1870. Yet a substantial number of Métis continued to live by hunting and trapping. The company sent out Protestant missionaries to join the Catholics already there in trying to persuade the Métis to settle down. But the clergymen achieved few results. "It was soon evident," recalled Ross, "that the habits of a lifetime were not to be overcome easily."

Twice a year, the residents of the Red River Colony threw their considerable energies into a buffalo hunt, an activity that assumed greater importance after several crop failures in the 1820s. The spring buffalo hunt, the larger of the two annual events, took on a major role in the economic life of the Hudson's Bay Company, as well as in the social life of the Métis. For the company, it became a source of pemmican, which was becoming harder and harder to obtain as the buffalo were depleted from the Canadian prairies. For the Métis, the hunt became the core of their community life and organization, with a degree of success that the Hudson's Bay Company had not expected and did not appreciate.

The large spring hunt involved a two-month expedition by as many as 1,000 people to the American prairies, 250 miles to the south, in present-day Minnesota or North Dakota, where there were still plenty of bison. As Alexander Ross described it: "With the earliest dawn of spring the hunters are in motion, like bees, and the colony in a state of confusion from their going to and fro. It is now that the company, the farmers, the petty traders are all beset by their incessant and irresistible importunities. One wants a horse, another an ax, a third a cart," and fully half of the purchases were made on credit, with payment promised after the hunt. "Thus the settlers are reluctantly drawn into profligate speculation—a system fraught with much evil, and ruinous alike to the giver and receiver of such favors." Yet such was the fervor to get on with the hunt, and so overwhelming was the number of participants, that to refuse credit would be, as Ross delicately put it, "not without risk."

After locating a herd of buffalo, the Métis set up camp and organized the

Using barrels for a goal, children play street hockey on an icy lot. Many Indian children also enjoy traditional entertainments, such as the cup-and-pin game played with bone and caribou-hide devices like the one shown at left.

hunt. Their hunting technique was at once thrilling and dangerous. Riders mounted on prized buffalo horses charged into the herd, each hunter maneuvering to within 10 feet or so of a fleeing bison, shooting it, and immediately seeking out another. A proficient hunter could kill as many as a dozen buffalo, one after the other, reloading his muzzleloading rifle on the gallop. "In less time than we have occupied with the description," wrote Ross, "a thousand carcasses strew the plain." Later, the women skinned and butchered the animals, and dried and processed most of the meat.

The Métis hunters loaded their bounty on their distinctive Red River carts—boxy wooden wagons with huge, six-foot-tall wooden wheels mounted on axles made of oak, all their pieces bound together with rawhide. The carts held about 800 pounds of freight, and drawn by oxen or horses, could travel about 20 miles a day. The wooden axles, grinding without benefit of lubrication against the wooden frames of the carts, creaked and groaned incessantly. One observer likened the noise to the "scraping of a thousand fingernails on a thousand panes of glass." It could be heard at a distance of three miles or more.

On their return to the Red River Colony, the buffalo hunters and their families indulged in an uproarious celebration, combining traditional Indian dances with Irish jigs and French reels. Musicians pounded Indian drums and sawed away on homemade fiddles tuned, it was jokingly said, to the "cry of the loon and the bellow of a rutting moose."

All this commotion was unsettling to government officials, the men of the church, and the barons of the Hudson's Bay Company. The number of participants in the buffalo hunts began to rise alarmingly. In 1820 a total of 540 carts left the colony on the spring hunt; by 1840 the number of carts had more than doubled, reaching 1,210. The white leadership was increasingly uncomfortable not only with the exuberance of the Métis hunters, and their substantial numbers, but also with the quasi-military organization they developed to protect themselves from hostile bands of Sioux Indians in whose territory they did their hunting. "Feeling their own strength, from being constantly armed, and free from control," Alexander Ross noted, the Métis "despise all others; but above all, they are marvelously tenacious of their own original habits." This was hardly what Lord Selkirk had envisioned as the civilizing effect of the Red River Colony.

Such habits were not restricted to the hunt but carried over into Métis life. Instead of devoting their Sundays to sober reflection on eternal verities, as their Catholic and Anglican mentors proposed, the Métis indulged in rounds of boisterous conviviality that included card games, gossip fests, horse races, and promenades. Even more unsettling to the authorities were those Métis who continued to trap and fish for their living and came to the settlement only occasionally.

But the most worrisome aspect of the Métis community was its size. By the end of the 1860s, as the new confederation of Canadian provinces was being crafted, the Métis outnumbered the white settlers in the Red River Colony by almost eight to one, making the mixed-bloods the largest community in the prospective new province of Manitoba.

The emergence of Canada as a self-governing dominion meant the end of Hudson's Bay Company control over the land. However difficult their relationship with the company had been, the Métis could not help but wonder whether the coming change in government, along with the expected influx of immigrants, would be for good or ill. Hunters wondered whether they would have enough territory to hunt. Those who held prop-

Gwich'ins from the Arctic Red River band play a guessing game. As one man shifts a small object from hand to hand, another guesses which hand holds the object. Other games involved gambling sticks, like the ones shown at top with their carrying case. The red and black markings denote the value of each stick.

erty, many without formal title, fretted about the new government's intention to stake off the land in squares and wondered what would happen to their off-sized, unrecorded lots.

In the summer of 1869, when the new government announced it was sending surveyors into the Red River country to lay out new townships, the Métis organized for resistance under the leadership of Montreal-educated Louis Riel, who spoke French and English, as well as Cree. They ordered the surveyors not to enter the colony. When the surveyors came anyway, Riel and his men drove them out and set up a provisional government in defiance of the Canadian authorities. To make sure that their rights and properties would be protected under the laws of the new confederation, a Métis committee submitted a list of provisions, which the Canadian Parliament incorporated in the legislation that created the province of Manitoba. In the summer of 1870, officials of the new province moved into the Red River Colony and took control. Fearing arrest and prosecution for his role in the brief rebellion, Louis Riel fled into Montana, where he spent the next 14 years teaching in a mission school.

Although the Manitoba Act reserved 1.4 million acres for ownership by the Métis, seven years passed before the government satisfied itself that it had properly identified the Métis eligible to claim the reserved land. And only then did the government begin issuing titles. In contrast, the white settlers who flocked to the area and staked out land obtained ownership documents quickly and easily.

Frustrated and angry, many Métis abandoned the Red River and set off to the north and west in search of a wilderness region where they could preserve their hunting and trapping life. But the days of the open frontier were fast coming to an end. The once vast herds of buffalo were disappearing rapidly. Group after group of western Indians were concluding treaties and moving onto reserves. Meanwhile, those Métis who had remained on their Red River farms continued to encounter roadblocks in getting title to their land and in gaining representation in the new Parliament.

Louis Riel returned to Canada in the summer of 1884. When the Red River Métis demanded that Riel represent them, the Canadian authorities were unreceptive. In the spring of 1885, Riel considered creating another provisional government. Canadian troops moved into the area to restore order. For a month, they were harassed by Métis guerrilla tactics and, in a battle at Cut Knife Hill, were forced to retreat by a combined force of Métis and Crees. After a period of time, however, the Métis fighters ran short of supplies and eventually were cornered at the village of Batoche, Saskatchewan, by a force of 700 soldiers. Riel surrendered on May 15. Six months later, despite appeals from around the world, he was hanged.

Nearly two decades after its merger with the North West Company, the Hudson's Bay Company had sufficiently reorganized its trading empire east of the Canadian Rockies to move beyond the great barrier into the last redoubts of the subarctic Indians—the areas known today as northwestern British Columbia, the Yukon Territory, and Alaska. There the company encountered bands that had been engaged for a century or more in trading with Russians. Only the Indians of the farthest reaches of Alaska—the Ingalik, Koyukon, and Tanaina—had been in direct contact with Russian traders, but their guns, knives, and blankets had moved to the southeast through middlemen. Indeed, before moving into the territory, the Hudson's Bay Company in 1838 bought out the rights of the Russian-American Company.

It was then that the Kaska Indians (whose territory lay across the present-day British Columbia-Yukon Territory border) first saw white traders—a Hudson's Bay Company party directed by Robert Campbell—

Tanaina grave houses rise like a miniature village from the graveyard of Saint Nicholas Orthodox Church in Eklutna, Alaska. Before the introduction of Christianity in the mid-1800s, the Tanaina cremated their dead.

paddling up the Liard River from the east. The Kaska were dominated by the Tlingit, a Northwest Coast people made up of various independent bands and noted for their proud warriors. The Tlingit had extended their trading franchise from the Peace to the Yukon Rivers. An influential Kaska woman chief befriended Campbell and his men, and tried to open trade with them, but could not overcome the hostility of the Tlingit. Campbell and his men persisted, optimistically building a trading post called Fort Selkirk at the junction of the Pelly and Yukon Rivers. But the competition turned violent. The Tlingit burned Campbell's post and drove the company traders temporarily from the region.

Of all the subarctic bands, the Koyukon lived farthest to the northwest, in north-central Alaska, and until 1847 had done their fur trading with Russians. But in that year, the Hudson's Bay Company built Fort Yukon, on

the northernmost arc of the Yukon River in east-central Alaska. The establishment of the trading post brought to its last frontier the now familiar pattern of the North American fur trade. The Koyukon quickly became dependent on manufactured goods and abandoned year-round subsistence hunting for the trapping of beaver, marten, and other furbearing animals. Soon they were trading not only to replace manufactured equipment but also to feed their families. Virtually all of the Koyukons began spending most of the summer at Fort Yukon, and many of the men left their families there, in permanent log houses, while they went out on winter trapping expeditions.

For a few more decades, a handful of the most isolated subarctic groups avoided prolonged contact with Europeans. The Tahltan, Tutchone, and Upper Tanana, for example, were either too far west of the Mackenzie River, too far south of the Yukon River, or too far inland from the Pacific Ocean for easy access to Hudson's Bay Company posts. This isolation was resolutely enforced by the Indians of the Pacific Northwest—the Ahtna, Tanaina, Tagish, and Chilkat—who aggressively blocked the incursions of white traders in order to retain their own roles as middlemen.

After 1850 the northern Athapaskans were subjected to another onslaught, this one against their sacred beliefs. For the previous three decades, the Hudson's Bay Company had refused to cooperate with missionaries, on the practical assumption that forcing the Indians to become Christian would do nothing to improve the company's take of beaver. But in 1851, French-speaking Roman Catholics of the Oblate order broke through this official secularism and established a mission on Lake Athabaska. From then on, the Oblates, along with a lesser number of Anglican missionaries, were an integral part of the fur trade. The priests moved through the subarctic bands, establishing missions and proselytizing until virtually every Indian was a nominal Christian.

But the days of insatiable demand for furs were over. In fact, although the company's profits varied widely from year to year, from 1840 on, there was a steady downward trend in the total number of pelts delivered (a decline that was reversed only briefly after 1853 when the company abandoned all pretense of protecting furbearing animals with quotas and seasons). Late in the century, however, the relatively languid pace of change accelerated dramatically for the bands living along the upper Yukon River. Frenzied competition returned with a vengeance, not for fur, but for a commodity regarded by the Indians as virtually useless—gold.

Two Lower Ahtna girls transport supplies and equipment by means of traditional pack straps called tumplines.

The Tahltan firebag (left), a moose-hide pouch attached to a red wool shoulder strap and decorated with beads and dentalium shells, contained equipment for starting fires like the metal, spark-making "strike-a-light" (inset).

For decades, the Chilkat Indians had prevented fur traders from passing over the Coast Mountains of northwestern British Columbia in order to preserve their franchise as middlemen. But in 1870, an adventurer named George Holt managed to get through. There was no point in trying to explain that he was not a threat to their fur trade, so Holt simply sneaked inland, over the 1,000-foot-high Chilkoot Pass into the basin of the Yukon River near the site of present-day Whitehorse. He found what he was looking for and carried it out in his pockets—two large gold nuggets.

Holt's find initiated a steadily growing stream of gold prospectors into the Yukon country. By 1886 some 200 had crossed Chilkoot Pass, and more had come overland from the Peace and Mackenzie River valleys. And they were but the vanguard. A flood of white men was about to engulf the area.

The quest for gold bewildered the Indians. They understood what fur traders wanted, and how to get it. However drastically the trade changed their lives, it was based on the familiar skills of hunting, trapping, and canoeing at which Indians excelled and white men were usually deficient.

The result was a mutual dependency that ameliorated conflicts between the two cultures. None of this was true of the gold rush. It drew white people in unprecedented numbers, in search of a metal whose attraction the Indians could not understand. Nor did they know how to find or extract it. Where the Indians had been indispensable to the fur trader, they were incidental to the goldminer.

The hide drum and drumstick (above left), eagle-quill ornaments (above, top), wooden rattle (above), and cedar-bark headdress (right) are ceremonial accouterments of the Carrier Indians of north-central British Columbia. They could have been used to celebrate the naming of an infant or the assumption of a family crest, or in the performance of ceremonies to honor the dead.

Yet many Indians found ways to benefit from this new white man's passion. After prospectors forced open the Chilkoot Pass, local Indians began to work as packers, bearing loads of up to 200 pounds and commanding rates that reached more than $100 a day. The wages were good enough to attract at least one white man, George Washington Carmack, an American from California who had married a Tagish woman and had been assimilated into Indian life.

In the summer of 1896, Carmack, his wife, and her two brothers went looking for trees to cut to sell as poles and lumber to prospectors on the Yukon River, 350 miles northwest of Chilkoot Pass. Carmack's small party went up a river called the Thron-Diuck, or "hammer-water," by the Indians, a reference to the stakes driven into the streambed for salmon nets. They encountered a prospector named Henderson and would have at-

tached themselves to him, but he had a bad attitude toward the Indians, so they elected to go their own way. That small decision altered the history of the West, for on August 17, on a stream soon to be renamed Bonanza Creek near the river whose name white men would pronounce as Klondike, they staked their claim and soon discovered gold.

Within two years, the news of the strike had spread around the world. By 1898 as many as 18,000 people lived in Dawson City, located at the junction of the Klondike and Yukon Rivers. The tide of prospectors overwhelmed the local Indians, who adapted to the new situation as best they could by working as guides, hunters, deck hands, woodcutters, cooks, cleaners, and porters. As the fur trade had done to other native groups, but with appalling speed and devastating effect, these jobs drew the Indians of the Yukon River away from their traditional pursuits into the tent cities of the gold prospectors, where they were exposed to disease, violence, alcohol, and alien ways of thinking.

When a Gwich'in Indian named Jarvis Mitchell walked south from his Porcupine River homeland into Fort Yukon in 1899, he found the town "full of people. I never saw so many. There were some kinds who talked languages I couldn't hear." But if the babbling foreigners amazed him, so did the Indians he encountered the next winter on a caribou hunt. There were "all kind of Indians up there," he marveled years later. The influx of whites had thrown the Indians together; relations between Indians from different groups had changed dramatically. Instead of exhibiting mistrust and suspicion, the various groups cooperated together. "Before we all hunt in different places," Mitchell recalled. "Old people used to be afraid of others. Now we don't care. Lots of times I give my meat to a Stick [Tutchone] Indian to sell for me. He never cheat me."

The Han Indians, whose traditional territory centered on the area of the biggest Klondike gold strikes, bore the brunt of the invasion. In the space of a few years, they changed dramatically. Many Hans began to dress as white men dressed, discarding their distinctive hairdos, nose decorations, and animal skins for cloth garments and hats; to reside, as did white men, in tents and wooden houses instead of structures of logs and hides; to travel in boats of plank and canvas instead of birch bark; to worship as Episcopalians. Other groups, such as the Koyukon and the Gwich'in, were deeply affected but managed to retain their identities.

The gold rush revealed an additional, stark difference between indigenous and European cultures. Indians valued goods for their utility, while white men seemed to measure everything by its worth in money. The fur trade had bridged this gap by expressing the price of goods and services in mutually understandable terms—beaver pelts. Sadly, there was no such correlation in the gold rush.

This cultural contrast was sharply drawn with the northwestern Athapaskan practice of the potlatch—a feast followed by the ceremonial giving of gifts by the host. The prestige of an Athapaskan leader frequently depended on the number and generosity of his potlatches. An Indian gained status by giving away, not accumulating, material things—a notion that seemed paradoxical to most Europeans.

The concept of paper currency was also alien to the Indians. Working or trading for a useful article or food was one thing, but why would one do it for little pieces of paper? Without warning, the gold rush imposed on everyone a cash economy. The Gwich'in who lived in the Peel River country north of the Klondike have a story called How the People Learned about Money. According to the tale, a party of white prospectors strayed into Gwich'in territory looking for a better way to the Klondike. The Gwich'in took pity on them and led them south to a pass leading to the gold-rush country. When the prospectors tried to pay for this service with cash, the Indians insisted on trade goods. Nevertheless, the white men handed out some samples of currency, which the Gwich'in regarded with amused contempt. On their way home they tore up or threw away most of the money, retaining only a few of the bills as curiosities. Much later, they were astonished when a trader spotted their souvenir money and offered to give them a wealth of trade goods in exchange. Immediately the Indians returned to the trail they had taken with the prospectors and scoured it for the money they had discarded along the way. The self-deprecating humor evident in the story served the Gwich'in well. They were able to preserve their identity throughout the gold rush to a degree unmatched by their neighbors to the south.

Within three years, the big gold strikes were mined out and more were not forthcoming. The gold rush ebbed as quickly as it had flowed. Some Han, Tutchone, Tanana, and Ahtna people went back to the fur trade and their hunting ways; others lived on the outskirts of white settlements cadging part-time and seasonal jobs.

The gold rush had been a brief, powerful outburst amid far-reaching and long-lasting change. The world economy had already turned away from commodities such as fur and had begun to concentrate on industrialization. The Canadian government, which had bought the lands chartered by the Hudson's Bay Company in 1869, was losing interest in sus-

Florence Albert, a Tanana elder, shares the stories of her people with archaeologist Theresa Villa. The numerous Tanana bands living along the Tanana River in western Alaska did not encounter whites until about 1880.

taining the fur trade. As far as the government was concerned, the future lay in building railroads across these lands, settling them, and exploiting their natural resources, including the rich mineral deposits.

In the face of these ambitious plans, the subarctic peoples were little more than an inconvenience. To be sure, there were humanitarian impulses at play in the creation of a national policy on Indian affairs, and there was sympathy for the sickness and poverty that threatened to wipe out the remnants of several groups. Sir Francis Bond Head, lieutenant governor of British Canada in the 1830s, believed that "the fate of the red inhabitants of America, the real proprietors of its soil, is, without any exception, the most sinful story recorded in the history of the human race." Convinced that they could not and would not become farmers, he advocated that the Indians be given land far from white settlements and allowed to live as they wished. As implemented, however, the policy accommodated the plans of the white settlers and the ideals of the white missionaries far more than the needs of the Indians.

The basic approach was established in an 1817 treaty with the Saulteaux Indians living near Lord Selkirk's Red River Colony. Successive, similar treaties were imposed on the bands living near the Great Lakes in the latter half of the 19th century and on the subarctic bands from Hudson Bay to the Mackenzie River during the first two decades of the 20th century.

"THE CARIBOU ARE OUR LIFE"

In mythic times, it is said among the Gwich'in, the people and the caribou lived together in harmony. Eventually, however, the people began to hunt the caribou. But the bonds between the hunter and the hunted only grew stronger. For thousands of years, the Gwich'in have depended on the animal not only for food, shelter, tools, and clothing but also as a source of spirituality. The Indians believe that a bit of human heart is in every caribou, and that a bit of caribou is in every person. Any threat to the animal is a threat to the Gwich'in. As one Gwich'in woman explains: "The caribou are our life. We must safeguard them forever."

In 1988, for the first time in more than 100 years, the many communities of the Gwich'in gathered at Arctic Village, Alaska, to discuss how to ensure their future as a people in the face of proposed oil and gas exploration inside the Arctic National Wildlife Refuge, birthing ground of the Porcupine caribou herd. Since then, the Gwich'in have held week-long gatherings every other year to celebrate their traditional heritage and to assess progress in the continuing fight to safeguard the animal that is the spiritual center of their life.

The timeless land of the Gwich'in stretches from Canada's Yukon Territory to Alaska's coastal plain. Artifacts found along Old Crow River suggest the region was home to the first people to reach the North American continent.

In 1994 Gwich'ins from all across the North came together in the Canadian village of Old Crow in the Yukon Territory (above) to debate the future of their ancient hunting culture. For days the talking stick, shown in the hand of Grafton Njootli (left), a Gwich'in leader from Old Crow, was passed from person to person until each participant had spoken. The Gwich'in pay special attention to the observations and ideas of elders like Sarah Able and Hannah Solomon (below).

Fabian Tritt from Arctic Village brings dancers onto the floor in a welcoming dance (above). The group at left is performing the Raven Dance. The dancers act out and tell stories about the feats and pranks of Raven, who is part culture hero and part trickster. Raven keeps the earth unsullied by cleaning up what is left behind by predators.

Honoring worthy individuals is an important component of every Gwich'in meeting. Playing tambourine-style drums, the singers (above) evoke spiritual power through their songs. Ovide Mercredi (right), first chief of the Assembly of First Nations, receives a new pair of moccasins as thanks for serving as keynote speaker. In the giveaway potlatch (below), the first gift is presented to Randall Tetlichi (being hugged) for his service in bringing spiritual peace to the community.

Although the Hudson's Bay Company provided for impoverished Indians in some areas of the North, it encouraged the treaties as a way of displacing its own responsibilities onto the Canadian government.

Government policy was to sequester the Indians on reserves. Successive groups of subarctic peoples were informed that in order to receive certain goods and services they would have to sign away all claims to their traditional territories. For a time, these agreements were called treaties, until—after the 1870s in the United States and the 1920s in Canada—the authorities became uncomfortable with the word's implication of a deal between sovereign nations.

In fact, of course, the typical treaty was hardly a deal between equals. "We told them," a treaty negotiator reported from Fort Garry on the Red River in 1871, "that whether they wished it or not, immigrants would come in and fill up the country; and that now was the time for them to come to an arrangement that would secure homes and amenities for themselves and their children." The announced intent of each treaty was to protect the Indians from harmful contact with white culture while providing them with enough healthcare, welfare, and education to stabilize their populations.

In its first comprehensive Indian Act of 1876, the Canadian government made clear that the reserves were to be temporary way stations on the road to complete assimilation. After settling down and converting to Christianity, an Indian would become eligible to apply for the vote. An enfranchised Indian would become a full citizen, at the price of renouncing all rights to ancestral lands.

In the meantime, the Indians would have to fit into categories devised by white Canadians. Athapaskan names were too difficult to pronounce and spell, so they were shortened and Anglicized. For government purposes, all Indians were placed in one of three categories: status Indians, who had certified membership in a registered band and were assigned a band number; treaty Indians, members of bands that had signed treaties and received an annual treaty payment; and nonstatus Indians, mostly Métis, who had no official status and received no benefits. The Indians living in areas where agriculture was possible were told that their survival depended on their ability to till the ground and grow crops.

This was a "complete reversal" of their way of life, wrote Edward Ahenakew, a Cree, and it was hardly surprising that many resisted farming, while many who tried it were completely unsuccessful. Only gradually did it dawn on the Indians that few other courses were open to them. "They did not realize that there was henceforward to be a definite system-

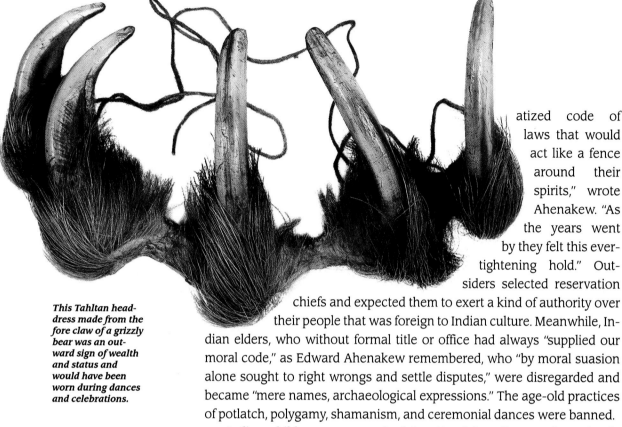

This Tahltan head-dress made from the fore claw of a grizzly bear was an outward sign of wealth and status and would have been worn during dances and celebrations.

atized code of laws that would act like a fence around their spirits," wrote Ahenakew. "As the years went by they felt this ever-tightening hold." Outsiders selected reservation chiefs and expected them to exert a kind of authority over their people that was foreign to Indian culture. Meanwhile, Indian elders, who without formal title or office had always "supplied our moral code," as Edward Ahenakew remembered, who "by moral suasion alone sought to right wrongs and settle disputes," were disregarded and became "mere names, archaeological expressions." The age-old practices of potlatch, polygamy, shamanism, and ceremonial dances were banned.

Indian children were required to attend boarding or day schools where they were sometimes punished for speaking their language, observing their customs, or remembering their history. During the 19th century, most of these schools were operated by the Roman Catholic or Anglican churches. At the turn of the 20th century, however, the Canadian government began supporting the mission schools and providing its own boarding schools and day schools.

In 1939, for the first time, the earnings generated by the fur trade in the Northwest Territories were surpassed by those of mining, lumbering, and oil. Also significant, especially in Alaska after the outbreak of World War II, were military operations and highway construction. But these activities generally depended on imported labor and brought little benefit to the native population. Worried about the Japanese threat in the North Pacific, the United States Army Corps of Engineers built the 1,500-mile-long Alaska Highway from Dawson Creek, British Columbia, to Big Delta, Alaska, southeast of Fairbanks. Along its length and across the Canadian West, other highways, oil pipelines, weather stations, and airfields, all part of the war effort, erupted with a local impact similar to that of the gold rush on the Klondike. In unexpected places, for about a decade, there would be a sudden abundance of jobs for Indians who could drive a truck, cook, pound a nail, or lift a burden. As before, the boom would end as quickly as it had begun, leaving the Indians no better off than they had been before.

When the military personnel and civilian workers who were part of the war effort in the North returned to their home communities, many spoke out about the squalid conditions of the northern peoples. They raised forceful questions about what they had seen and whether their governments should be doing more to help.

In addition to specific legislation aimed at Indians, the Canadian and provincial governments increasingly included Indians in programs designed to improve the well-being of the general population. Beginning in the 1940s and continuing through the 1950s and 1960s, more schools and public housing were built. In addition, the Indians received improved healthcare and welfare benefits—including a federal allowance for each child and pensions for the elderly—and became eligible to vote in provincial elections. Death rates declined, school populations increased, and living standards improved. Between 1941 and 1970, the number of Athapaskan Indians living near trading posts increased by 56 percent.

Yet chronic problems persisted. A profound grief at the loss of self-sufficiency has often overshadowed the efforts of the subarctic peoples to come to terms with the disadvantages and opportunities presented by increased contact with modern society and its institutions. Schools pulled children from their families and the old ways; government classifications threatened identities; public housing anchored people to settlements where there were no jobs.

By the middle of the 20th century, the Hudson's Bay Company outposts had become general stores (later, in the larger cities, department stores) rather than trading posts. Yet despite all the pressures to the contrary, the fur trade continued to be the occupation of choice for many subarctic Indians. During the 1960s and 1970s, as fur profits declined, federal and provincial programs supported trapping. Meanwhile, the spread of radio, television, and newspapers brought information about the standard of living in America and Canada, which had the effect—just as had the first awareness of metal tools and guns—of raising aspirations. But this time, there was no product or service the Indian could offer to fulfill these new dreams.

A century after the institution of the reservation policy, there emerged in Alaska and northwestern Canada several movements uniting groups of indigenous peoples in asserting their claims to traditional lands. The first of these to emerge was the Alaska Federation of Natives, organized in 1967 by representatives of various Indian, Aleut, and Eskimo groups in the state. In the economic boom that began after the discovery of vast oil and gas reserves beneath the North Slope of the Brooks Range, the local inhabi-

Residents of a Koyukon village on the lower Yukon River dance around a pole draped with furs during the Stick Dance, a major event of the memorial potlatch hosted by the family and friends of the deceased to honor their loved one's life and thank those who helped at the time of death.

tants pointed out that while the U.S. government had come to an agreement with Russia when it acquired the territory in 1867, it had never bothered to consult with them about ownership of the land and its resources. Yet they had continuously occupied, and claimed title to, about 90 percent of Alaska. In 1971 they won a cash settlement of $500 million and a two percent royalty on all oil and mineral revenues derived from their territory.

The Alaskan agreement stimulated the formation of political action organizations among other native groups not restricted by specific treaties—the Union of British Columbia Chiefs, for example, and the Indian Brotherhoods of the Prairie Provinces and Territories of Canada. By coordinating their votes and learning modern public relations techniques, these organizations became a potent force for reform of government policy toward the Indians, and for preservation of traditional land rights and culture. In 1973 the Canadian government began to negotiate land claims in which Indian groups reasserted their ownership of huge tracts of land in British Columbia, the Northwest Territories, northern Quebec, and Labrador. On these re-claimed lands, with a new share in the revenues derived from them, many Indian groups began to reestablish their culture and redefine the ways in which they wanted to live alongside the majority culture.

In the summer of 1975, members of the Mackenzie River bands (who, like other modern Athapaskans, refer to themselves as Dene) addressed a Canadian government commission considering their objections to the building of a natural-gas pipeline along the length of the river. The Dene speakers described the detrimental effects of the proposed pipeline and asserted their rights to ownership of the land as well as their rights to self-determination as an independent nation.

And one of them, a Dene social worker from Fort McPherson by the name of Phillip Blake, explained to the commission the benefits white society could derive from changing the pattern of exploitation that was now more than four centuries old. "For thousands of years, we have lived with the land," Blake told the commission, "we have taken care of the land, and the land has taken care of us. We have been satisfied to see our wealth as ourselves and the land we live with. It is our greatest wish to be able to pass on this land to succeeding generations in the same condition that our fathers have given it to us." This way of life is worth preserving, Blake argued, for the sake not only of Indian people but of white civilization as well. "I believe that your nation might wish to see us, not as a relic from the past, but as a way of life, a system of values by which you may survive in the future. This we are willing to share." ✦

Holding his catch in a net, a Cree fisherman solemnly observes the reflection of Hydro-Quebec's power plant on the La Grande River. A series of dams built for the complex led to the flooding of some of the most productive Cree lands in the James Bay region.

Early each spring, the Ingalik of the Yukon and Kusko-kwim River basins began preparations for the Mask Dance. One of seven major Ingalik ceremonies, the Mask Dance was performed to honor the animal spirits so that they would send fish and food-giving mammals to the people in the coming year. It was also an occasion for fun and fellowship—and an opportunity to enjoy the prestige of giving generously.

After a date had been set for the celebration, old masks were refurbished and new ones begun. Any man who had had a dream about an animal since the last Mask Dance was allowed to carve a mask, using clear-grained green spruce he had cut from the forest. The new masks might require new songs, composed in order to foster good relations with the animal spirits. Creatures such as salmon, caribou, grouse, owl, fox, porcupine, crane, and raven, as well as human beings, were represented in the

masks, which were painted, decorated with feathers, and sometimes given hinged appendages.

When all the preparations had been completed, masked messengers set off to invite a neighboring village to share in the festivities. Two days later, the guests arrived and were greeted as they approached by the hosts, who were led by the messengers howling like wolves. The whole party proceeded to the kashim, or ceremonial house, where the visitors received refreshments and rested after their journey. Later, each guest was taken to the home of a resident for dinner. After the meal, all were summoned to the kashim for a series of dances, each one characterized by graceful, rhythmic movements. While both men and women participated in the dancing, only the men could wear the face masks. At the conclusion of the ceremony, gifts were presented to the guests and everyone left the kashim to participate in a feast.

Some of the many animal and human masks used during the Mask Dance are displayed on the outer wall of a kashim (below) in Anvik, Alaska, about the end of the 19th century.

The Half-Man mask at right was made by a man who had a dream about a creature with only half a body who lived inside a mountain. The dancer made a distinctive noise through the circular mouth, suggesting communication with the spirit world.

MESSENGERS
AND STRANGERS
FROM AFAR

The mouth of the one-eyed Messenger mask (right) was originally stuffed with a squirrel skin as an indication of its favorite food.

The small mask at left was used by the messengers to invite guests to the Mask Dance. The smiling mouth may have represented a man.

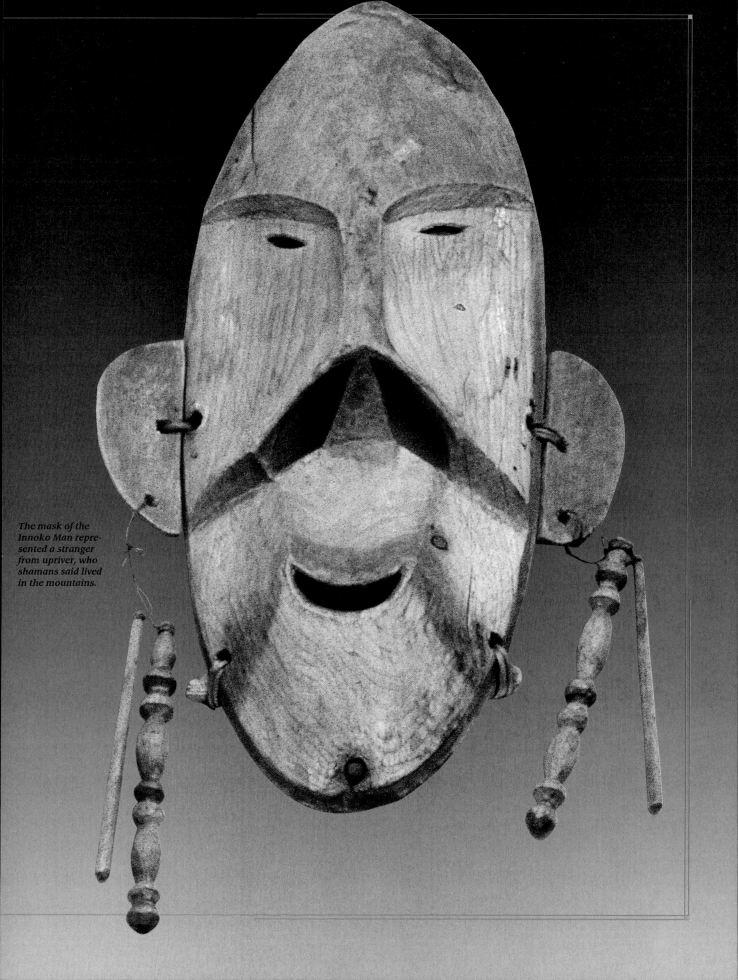

The mask of the Innoko Man represented a stranger from upriver, who shamans said lived in the mountains.

CREATURES
OF THE AIR
AND WATER

The Raven (above left), Crow (left), and Ruffed Grouse (below) all performed in a set of bird dances. A 1905 observer credited the wearer of the Grouse mask with offering a "capital representation of the motions of a grouse."

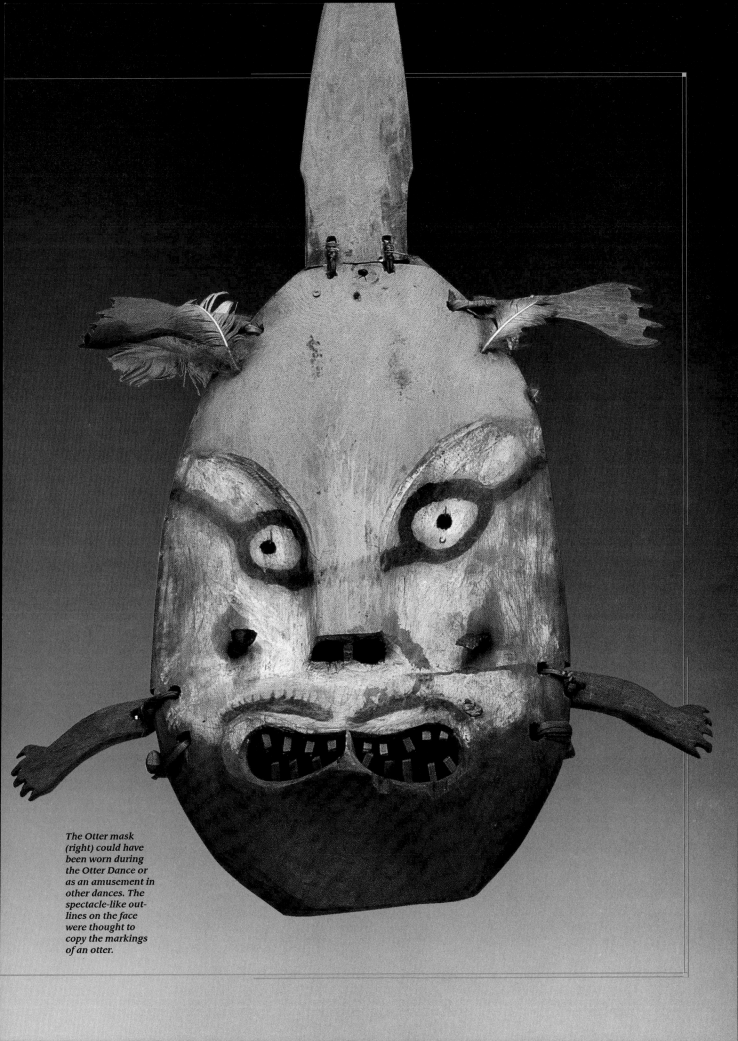

The Otter mask (right) could have been worn during the Otter Dance or as an amusement in other dances. The spectacle-like outlines on the face were thought to copy the markings of an otter.

ACKNOWLEDGMENTS

The editors wish to thank the following individuals and institutions for their valuable assistance:

In Canada:
British Columbia—Dan Savard, Royal British Columbia Museum, Victoria. Manitoba—Maureen Dolyniuk, Debra Moore, Hudson's Bay Company Archives, Provincial Archives of Manitoba; Mary Ann Tisdale, Canadian Heritage-Parks, Winnipeg. Northwest Territories—Chief Dennis Deneron, Trout Lake; Shirley Lamalice-Camsell, Hay River. Ontario—Harvey Feit, McMaster University, Hamilton; Edwidge Munn, National Archives of Canada; Boyce Richardson, Ottawa. Quebec—Tony Ianzelo, National Film Board of Canada, Montreal; Neil Jotham, Canadian Wildlife Service; Diane Reid, Cree Regional Authority, Chateauguay; Margery Toner, Museum of Civilization, Hull.

In the United States:
Alaska: Anchorage—Donna Carroll, Robert Childers, The Gwich'in Steering Committee; Raymond Solomon.
Arizona: Tempe—Kate C. Duncan, Arizona State University.
Washington State: Seattle—Rebecca Andrews, The Burke Museum; Carolyn Marr, The Museum of History and Industry; Nancy Hines, Stan Shockey, University of Washington; Richard H. Engeman, John Medlin, University of Washington Libraries; Janet Anderson. Spokane—Brother Ed. Jennings, S.J., Sharon M. Prendergast, Gonzaga University Library. Tacoma—Elaine Miller, Joy Werlink, Washington State Historical Society.

BIBLIOGRAPHY

BOOKS

Alberta Federation of Metis Settlement Associations, Daniel R. Anderson, and Alda M. Anderson. *The Metis People of Canada: A History.* Toronto: Gage Publishing, 1978.

America's Fascinating Indian Heritage. Pleasantville, N.Y.: Reader's Digest Association, 1978.

Armitage, Peter. *The Innu.* New York: Chelsea House Publishers, 1991.

Bailey, Alfred Goldsworthy. *The Conflict of European and Eastern Algonkian Cultures, 1504-1700: A Study in Canadian Civilization.* Toronto: University of Toronto Press, 1969.

Bicchieri, M. G., ed. *Hunters and Gatherers Today: A Socioeconomic Study of Eleven Such Cultures in the Twentieth Century.* New York: Holt, Rinehart and Winston, 1972.

Biggar, Henry Percival. *The Early Trading Companies of New France.* St. Clair Shores, Mich.: Scholarly Press, 1972 (reprint of 1901 edition).

Bishop, Charles A. *The Northern Ojibwa and the Fur Trade: An Historical and Ecological Study.* Toronto: Holt, Rinehart and Winston of Canada, 1974.

Brasser, Ted J. *"Bo'jou, Neejee!"* Ottawa, Ont.: National Museum of Man, 1976.

Brightman, Robert. *Grateful Prey: Rock Cree Human-Animal Relationships.* Berkeley: University of California Press, 1993.

Brody, Hugh. *Living Arctic: Hunters of the Canadian North.* Seattle: University of Washington Press, 1990.

Brown, Jennifer S. H. *Strangers in Blood: Fur Trade Company Families in Indian Country.* Vancouver: University of British Columbia Press, 1980.

Brown, Jennifer S. H., and Robert Brightman. *"The Orders of the Dreamed": George Nelson on Cree and Northern Ojibwa Religion and Myth, 1823.* St. Paul: Minnesota Historical Society Press, 1988.

Canada's Native Peoples. Vol. 2 of *Canada Heirloom Series.* Mississauga, Ont.: Heirloom Publishing, 1988.

Chapman, John W. "Notes on the Tinneh Tribe of Anvik, Alaska." In *Congrès International des Américanistes, 15th Session.* Vol. 2. Quebec City: Dussault & Proulx, 1907.

Colombo, John Robert, ed. *Windigo: An Anthology of Fact and Fantastic Fiction.* Saskatoon, Sask.: Western Producer Prairie Books, 1982.

Crowe, Keith J. *A History of the Original Peoples of Northern Canada.* Montreal, Que.: McGill-Queen's University Press, 1991.

Cumming, Peter A., and Neil H. Mickenberg, eds. *Native Rights in Canada.* Toronto: The Indian-Eskimo Association of Canada, 1972.

Daniells, Roy. *Alexander Mackenzie and the North West.* New York: Barnes & Noble, 1969.

Duncan, Kate C. *Northern Athapaskan Art: A Beadwork Tradition.* Seattle: University of Washington Press, 1989.

Dunning, Robert William. *Social and Economic Change among the Northern Ojibwa.* Toronto: University of Toronto Press, 1959.

Ewing, Douglas C. *Pleasing the Spirits: A Catalogue of a Collection of American Indian Art.* New York: Ghylen Press, 1982.

Garbarino, Merwyn S. *Native American Heritage.* Prospect Heights, Ill.: Waveland Press, 1985.

Gilman, Carolyn. *Where Two Worlds Meet: The Great Lakes Fur Trade.* St. Paul: Minnesota Historical Society, 1982.

Hail, Barbara A., and Kate C. Duncan. *Out of the North: The Subarctic Collection of the Haffenreffer Museum of Anthropology.* Bristol, R.I.: Haffenreffer Museum of Anthropology, 1989.

Hallowell, A. Irving. *The Role of Conjuring in Saulteaux Society.* Vol. 2. New York: Octagon Books, 1971 (reprint of 1942 edition).

Harrison, Julia D. *Metis: People between Two Worlds.* Vancouver, B.C.: Glenbow-Alberta Institute, 1985.

Helm, June, ed. *Subarctic.* Vol. 6 of *Handbook of North American Indians.* Washington, D.C.: Smithsonian Institution, 1981.

Innis, Harold A. *The Fur Trade in Canada: An Introduction to Canadian Economic History.* Toronto: University of Toronto Press, 1956.

Jenness, Diamond. *The Indians of Canada.* Toronto: University of Toronto Press, 1977.

Journals of Samuel Hearne and Philip Turnor between the Years 1774 and 1792. New York: Greenwood Press, 1968.

Judd, Carol M., and Arthur J. Ray, eds. *Old Trails and New Directions: Papers of the Third North American Fur Trade Conference.* Toronto: University of Toronto Press, 1980.

Krech, Shepard, III, ed.:
Indians, Animals, and the Fur Trade: A Critique of Keepers of the Game. Athens: University of Georgia Press, 1981.
The Subarctic Fur Trade: Native Social and Economic Adaptations. Vancouver: University of British Columbia Press, 1984.

Leacock, Eleanor B., and Nan A. Rothschild, eds. *Labrador Winter: The Ethnographic Journals of William Duncan Strong, 1927-1928.* Washington, D.C.: Smithsonian Institution Press, 1994.

MacDonald, Robert. *The Owners of Eden: The Life and Past of the Native People.* Calgary, Alta.: Ballantrae Foundation, 1974.

McDonald, T. H., ed. *Exploring the Northwest Territory.* Norman: University of Oklahoma Press, 1966.

McMillan, Alan D. *Native Peoples and Cultures of Canada: An Anthropological Overview.* Vancouver, B.C.: Douglas & McIntyre, 1988.

Metis Association of Alberta, et al. *Metis Land Rights in Alberta: A Political History.* Edmonton: Metis Association of Alberta, 1981.

Moore, James T. *Indian and Jesuit: A Seventeenth-Century Encounter.* Chicago: Loyola University Press, 1982.

Morrison, R. Bruce, and C. Roderick Wilson. *Native Peoples: The Canadian Experience.* Toronto: McClelland and Stewart, 1986.

National Museum of Man. *The Athapaskans: Strangers of the North.* Ottawa, Ont.: National Museum of Man, 1974.

Native American Myths and Legends. New York: Smithmark Publishers, 1994.

Osgood, Cornelius:
Contributions to the Ethnography of the Kutchin. New Haven, Conn.: Yale University Press, 1936.
The Han Indians: A Compilation of Ethnographic and Historical Data on the Alaska-Yukon Boundary Area. New Haven, Conn.: Yale University Press, 1971.
Ingalik Social Culture. New Haven, Conn.: Yale University Press, 1958.

Osgood, William, and Leslie Hurley. *The Snowshoe Book.* Brattleboro, Vt.: Stephen Greene Press, 1983.

Patterson, E. Palmer, II. *The Canadian Indian: A History Since 1500.* Don Mills, Ont.: Collier-Macmillan Canada, 1972.

Price, John A. *Indians of Canada: Cultural Dynamics.* Scarborough, Ont.: Prentice-Hall of Canada, 1979.

Ray, Arthur J. *Indians in the Fur Trade: Their Role as Trappers, Hunters, and Middlemen in the Lands Southwest of Hudson Bay, 1660-1870.* Toronto: University of Toronto Press, 1974.

Ray, Arthur J., and Donald B. Freeman. *'Give Us Good Measure': An Economic Analysis of Relations between the Indians and the Hudson's Bay Company before 1763.* Toronto: University of Toronto Press, 1978.

Roberts, Kenneth G., and Philip Shackleton. *The Canoe: A History of the Craft from Panama to the Arctic.* Camden, Maine: International Marine Publishing, 1983.

Rogers, Edward S.:
The Material Culture of the Mistassini. Ottawa, Ont.: National Museum of Canada, 1967.
The Round Lake Ojibwa. Toronto: Ontario Department of Lands and Forests, 1962.

Ross, Alexander. *The Red River Settlement: Its Rise, Progress, and Present State.* Rutland, Vt.: Charles E. Tuttle, 1972.

Sealey, D. Bruce. *Cuthbert Grant and the Métis* (We Built Canada series). Agincourt, Ont.: Book Society of Canada, 1976.

Simeone, William E. *A History of Alaskan Athapaskans.* [Anchorage]: Alaska Historical Commission, 1983.

Speck, Frank G. *Naskapi: The Savage Hunters of the Labrador Peninsula.* Norman: University of Oklahoma Press, 1977.

The Spirit Sings: Artistic Traditions of Canada's First Peoples. Toronto: McClelland and Stewart, 1987.

Steltzer, Ulli. *Indian Artists at Work.* Vancouver, B.C.: Douglas & McIntyre, 1976.

Stevens, James R. *Sacred Legends of the Sandy Lake Cree.* Toronto: McClelland and Stewart, 1971.

Tanner, Adrian. *Bringing Home Animals: Religious Ideology and Mode of Production of the Mistassini Cree Hunters.* New York: St. Martin's Press, 1979.

Thwaites, Reuben Gold, ed. *The Jesuit Relations and Allied Documents: Travels and Explorations of the Jesuit Missionaries in New France, 1610-1791.* Vols. 5, 6, and 7. Cleveland: Burrows Brothers, 1897.

Trudel, Marcel. *The Beginnings of New France: 1524-1663.* Trans. by Patricia Claxton. Toronto: McClelland and Stewart, 1973.

Turner, Lucien M. "Ethnology of the Ungava District in Hudson Bay Territory." In *Eleventh Annual Report of the Bureau of Ethnology.* Washington, D.C.: Government Printing Office, 1894.

Tyrrell, J. B., ed. *David Thompson's Narrative of His Explorations in Western America: 1784-1812.* Toronto: Champlain Society, 1916.

Van Kirk, Sylvia. *Many Tender Ties: Women in Fur-Trade Society, 1670-1870.* Norman: University of Oklahoma Press, 1980.

Vanstone, James W. *Athapaskan Adaptations.* Chicago: Aldine Publishing, 1974.

Watkins, Mel, ed. *Dene Nation: The Colony Within.* Toronto: University of Toronto Press, 1977.

Whymper, Frederick. *Travel and Adventure in the Territory of Alaska.* Ann Arbor, Mich.: University Microfilms, 1966.

Yerbury, J. C. *The Subarctic Indians and the Fur Trade, 1680-1860.* Vancouver: University of British Columbia Press, 1986.

PERIODICALS

Bishop, Charles A. "Windigo: Cannibal Myth of North American Indians." *Field Museum of Natural History Bulletin,* September 1973.

Clark, Annette McFadyen, and Donald W. Clark. "Koyukon Athapaskan Houses as Seen through Oral Tradition and through Archaeology." *Arctic Anthropology,* 1974.

Cooke, Alan. "The Montagnais." *The Beaver,* Summer 1983.

Cooper, John M. "The Cree Witiko Psychosis." *Primitive Man,* January 1933.

Dailey, R. C. "The Role of Alcohol among North American Indian Tribes as Reported in the Jesuit Relations." *Anthropologica,* January 1968.

Flannery, Regina:
"Cross-Cousin Marriage among the Cree and Montagnais of James Bay." *Primitive Man,* 1938.
"The Shaking-Tent Rite among the Montagnais of James Bay." *Primitive Man,* January 1939.

Garrett, W. E. "Canada's Heartland: The Prairie Provinces." *National Geographic,* October 1970.

Hessel, Peter. "The Algonkins of Golden Lake." *The Beaver,* Winter 1983.

Kroul, Mary V. "Definitional Domains of the Koyukon Athapaskan Potlatch. *Arctic Anthropology,* 1974.

McKennan, Robert A. "The Chandalar Kutchin." *Arctic Institute of North America Technical Paper* (Montreal), September 1965.

Mitchell, John G. "James Bay: Where Two Worlds Collide." *National Geographic,* November 1993.

Reynolds, Brad. "Athapaskans along the Yukon." *National Geographic,* February 1990.

Slobodin, Richard. " 'The Dawson Boys'—Peel River Indians and the Klondike Gold Rush." *Polar Notes* (Dartmouth College Library, Hanover, N.H.), June 1963.

Ward, Fred. "The Changing World of Canada's Crees." *National Geographic,* April 1975.

Williams, Glyndwr. "The Hudson's Bay Company and the Fur Trade: 1670-1870. *The Beaver,* Autumn 1983.

OTHER SOURCES

"Gwich'in Niintsyaa: The 1988 Arctic Village Gathering." Video recording. Anchorage, Alaska: Gwich'in Steering Committee, 1988.

Ottereyes, Eva, Joseph Ottereyes, and Harvey Feit. "Photographs of a Shaking Tent Ceremony: Waswanipi Region of Quebec, October 22-25, 1969." Photographs captioned and labeled. Hamilton, Ont.: McMaster University, August 1982.

PICTURE CREDITS

Oklahoma Library. **39:** Courtesy Smithsonian Institution, *Handbook of North American Indians*, Vol. 6, after J. Alden Mason, "Notes on the Indians of the Great Slave Lake Area," *Yale University Publications in Anthropology*, 34, New Haven, 1946. **40:** Yukon Archives/MacBride Museum Collection/print no. 3869. **41:** Courtesy Smithsonian Institution, *Handbook of North American Indians*, Vol. 6, after Annette McFadyen Clark and Donald W. Clark, "Koyukon Athapaskan Houses as Seen through Oral Tradition and through Archaeology," *Arctic Anthropology*, 11 (suppl.): 29-38. **42, 43:** Bryan and Cherry Alexander, Sturminster Newton, Dorset. **44:** Nellie Cadzow Carroll. **45:** The McCord Museum of Canadian History, Montreal, #ME 966X.111.7 & .8. **46:** Courtesy Royal Ontario Museum, Toronto, neg. no. 986.218.1. **49-51:** Harvey A. Feit. **52:** British Columbia Archives and Records Service, cat. no. 75357—Robin Ridington. **53:** Canadian Museum of Civilization, Hull, neg. no. 33085. **54, 55:** Courtesy Thomas Burke Memorial Washington State Museum, cat. nos. BWSM 2646; 2644. **57:** Beryl G. Gillespie. **58:** Hudson's Bay Company Archives, Provincial Archives of Manitoba—Canadian Museum of Civilization, Hull, neg. no. S75-4233. **59:** National Museum of Natural History, Smithsonian Institution, no. 248388—Canadian Museum of Civilization, Hull, neg. no. S75-4234. **60:** Special Collections Division, University of Washington Libraries, neg. no. NA 2911—Hudson's Bay Company Archives, Provincial Archives of Manitoba. **61:** Provincial Archives of Alberta, Ernest Brown Collection, neg. no. B.923. **63:** "Windigo," Norval Morrisseau, Glenbow Collection, Calgary. **64-71:** Background courtesy Huntley Meadows Park, Alexandria, Virginia. **64, 65:** Neg. no. 4976 (photo by Don Eiler), Department of Library Services, American Museum of Natural History; Boyce Richardson. **66:** Boyce Richardson—William J. Hennessy Jr. of A & W Graphics Ltd. **67:** Boyce Richardson. **68, 69:** National Film Board of Canada, Montreal; Boyce Richardson (except top left). **70, 71:** National Film Board of Canada, Montreal; Boyce Richardson (except top left). **72-79:** Background by Denver Art Museum. **72, 73:** Adrian Tanner. **74, 75:** Boyce Richardson—Harvey A. Feit; National Film Board of Canada, Montreal—neg. no. 4976 (photo by Don Eiler), Department of Library Services, American Museum of Natural History. **76:** National Film Board of Canada, Montreal. **77:** © Adrian Tanner/VidéAnthrop—trans. no. 4976 (photo by Don Eiler), Department of Library Services, American Museum of Natural History (2). **78:** National Film Board of Canada, Montreal—© Adrian Tanner/VidéAnthrop; © Fred Ward. **79:** Boyce Richardson. **80, 81:** Department of Canadian Heritage, Professional & Technical Services, Prairie & Northwest Territories Region—courtesy Royal Ontario Muse-

um, Toronto. **82:** The Huntington Library. **83:** © DeLongeville/Publiphoto. **85:** Minnesota Historical Society. **86, 87:** Map by Maryland CartoGraphics, Inc.—National Archives of Canada, Ottawa, trans. no. C-1920. **88:** National Archives of Canada, Ottawa, neg. no. PA-147466—Canadian Museum of Civilization, Hull, trans. no. S75-4116. **89:** National Archives of Canada, Ottawa, neg. no. PA-144223—Bryan and Cherry Alexander, Sturminster Newton, Dorset. **90:** Bryan and Cherry Alexander, Sturminster Newton, Dorset. **91:** Courtesy Royal Ontario Museum, Toronto. **93:** Olaus J. Murie, National Archives of Canada, Ottawa, neg. no. PA-136291—National Archives of Canada, Ottawa, trans. no. C-033689. **95, 97:** Hudson's Bay Company Archives, Provincial Archives of Manitoba. **98, 99:** Courtesy Royal Ontario Museum, Toronto. **101:** National Archives of Canada, Ottawa. **103:** Denver Art Museum. **104:** Wilbur E. Garrett, © National Geographic Society. **105:** © Winston Fraser/Fraser Photos. **107:** Sydney Prior Hall, National Archives of Canada, Ottawa, neg. no. C-12984—© Winston Fraser/Fraser Photos. **108, 109:** Department of Canadian Heritage, Professional & Technical Services, Prairie & Northwest Territories Region. **110:** Bryan and Cherry Alexander, Sturminster Newton, Dorset—Canadian Museum of Civilization, Hull, trans. no. S75-4167. **111:** Collected by S. B. McLenegan, LMA-10889, photograph courtesy Phoebe A. Hearst Museum of Anthropology, University of California at Berkeley. **112:** Kate Duncan photographer, Smithsonian Institution, trans. no. 15757—courtesy Thomas Burke Memorial Washington State Museum—Milwaukee Public Museum. **113:** Provincial Museum of Alberta, Edmonton, trans. no. 73-55. 1a-c. **114:** Haffenreffer Museum of Anthropology, Brown University, neg. no. 57-514—Royal British Columbia Museum, Victoria, cat. no. 2913. **115:** Kate Duncan, photographer, Royal British Columbia Museum, Victoria—Canadian Museum of Civilization, Hull, trans. no. S84-5992. **116, 117:** Bryan and Cherry Alexander, Sturminster Newton, Dorset—James Trapper, Waskaganish, Quebec, courtesy The Snow Goose, Ottawa; © Fred Ward. **118:** Bryan and Cherry Alexander, Sturminster Newton, Dorset. **119:** © Ted Levin. **120:** J. Russell, National Archives of Canada, Ottawa, neg. no. PA-19988. **121:** Jim Yuskavitch. **122:** Minnesota Historical Society, trans. no. 68.97.1—courtesy Glenbow Archives, Calgary, Alberta, neg. no. NA-949-83. **123:** Hudson's Bay Company Archives, Provincial Archives of Manitoba, neg. no. N8347. **124, 125:** Haffenreffer Museum of Anthropology, Brown University, photo by Cathy Carver—courtesy Royal Ontario Museum, Toronto; Nicholas C. P. Vrooman, Institute of Metis Studies, College of Great Falls, Montana, from the Minnesota Historical Society, neg. no. 405—National Archives of Canada, Ottawa,

neg. no. PA-46110. **126, 127:** National Archives of Canada, Ottawa, neg. no. C-81767—Canadian Museum of Civilization, Hull, trans. no. S85-1312; courtesy Royal Ontario Museum, Toronto. **128, 129:** Courtesy Nicholas C. P. Vrooman, Institute of Metis Studies, College of Great Falls, Montana (2)—Sydney Prior Hall, National Archives of Canada, Ottawa, neg. no. C-12997. **130, 131:** Courtesy Glenbow Archives, Calgary, Alberta, neg. no. AC 335—Buffalo Bill Historical Center, Cody, Wyoming, gift of Olin Corporation, Winchester Arms Collection—photo by William Firth, Northwest Territories Metis Nation; courtesy Glenbow Archives, Calgary, Alberta, neg. nos. PA-2218-26—PA-2218-202. **132:** Mike Kesterton—New Breed Magazine, Metis Nation of Saskatchewan—Doug Curran. **133:** Courtesy Nicholas C. P. Vrooman, Institute for Metis Studies, College of Great Falls, Montana, photo by Murray Lemley. **134:** Canadian Museum of Civilization, Hull, neg. no. S75-4096—Sherman Hines/Masterfile. **136, 137:** Provincial Archives of Alberta, Ernest Brown Collection, no. B.779; Bryan and Cherry Alexander, Sturminster Newton, Dorset. **138:** National Archives of Canada, Ottawa, neg. no. PA-17947. **139:** Bryan and Cherry Alexander, Sturminster Newton, Dorset. **140:** National Archives of Canada, Ottawa, neg. no. C-8953. **141:** Sherman Hines/Masterfile. **143:** Erik Hill/Anchorage Daily News. **144:** National Archives of Canada, Ottawa, neg. no. PA 42048—from the collection of Frederica de Laguna. **145:** Erik Hill/Anchorage Daily News. **146:** National Archives of Canada, Ottawa, neg. no. C-8951; courtesy Thomas Burke Memorial Washington State Museum. **147:** Courtesy Thomas Burke Memorial Washington State Museum; from *Indian Artist at Work* by Ulli Steltzer, Douglas and McIntyre, Vancouver, 1976. **148, 149:** National Archives of Canada, Ottawa, neg. no. C-20851; C-37311. **150:** Canadian Museum of Civilization, Hull, trans. no. S75-4223. **151:** David Falconer and Associates. **153:** J. F. Moran, National Archives of Canada, Ottawa, trans. no. PA-102486—courtesy Thomas Burke Memorial Washington State Museum. **155:** Wolfgang Kaehler. **156:** Courtesy Thomas Burke Memorial Washington State Museum; Royal British Columbia Museum, Victoria. **157:** NAA, Smithsonian Institution, neg. no. 75-5648. **158, 159:** Courtesy Thomas Burke Memorial Washington State Museum. **161:** Jim Yuskavitch. **162-165:** Ray Solomon. **167:** Courtesy Thomas Burke Memorial Washington State Museum. **169:** Don Doll, S.J. **170, 171:** Stephenie Hollyman/Gamma Liaison. **172:** NAA, Smithsonian Institution, neg. no. 10455-N-1. **173:** Trans. no. 1983(3) (photo by Don Eiler), Department of Library Services, American Museum of Natural History. **174-177:** Trans. no. 4975(2) (photo by Don Eiler), Department of Library Services, American Museum of Natural History.